How Can We Know?

How Can We Know?

A. N. Wilson

IMAGE BOOKS
DOUBLEDAY
NEW YORK LONDON TORONTO SYDNEY AUCKLAND

An Image Book
PUBLISHED BY DOUBLEDAY
a division of Bantam Doubleday Dell Publishing Group, Inc.
666 Fifth Avenue, New York, New York 10103

IMAGE, and DOUBLEDAY are trademarks of Doubleday,
a division of Bantam Doubleday Dell Publishing Group, Inc.

This Image Books edition published September 1991 by
special arrangement with Macmillan Publishing Company.

Library of Congress Cataloging-in-Publication Data
Wilson, A. N., 1950–
    How can we know? / A. N. Wilson.
        p.   cm.
    Reprint. Originally published: New York:
Atheneum, 1985. "An Image Book."
    1. Apologetics—20th century.   I. Title.
[BT1102.W55   1991]   91-13228
239—dc20   CIP
ISBN 0-385-41960-0

Contents

In creative writing, most rules are regarded as flexible, and may — knowingly but never unknowingly — be bent or stretched to suit the writer's purpose. The word, the sentence, the paragraph, all have as their primary function the creation of a mood or an impression. They must suggest far more than they actually say, for it is by the power of suggestion that they stimulate the imagination or stir the emotions of the reader.

Preface

Thomas the Twin, sometimes called Doubting Thomas, is an attractive voice in the Gospels. In the great discourse towards the end of John's Gospel, Jesus tells his friends that he is going away to prepare a place for them, and that they all know both where he is going and the way he is going. It is Thomas who answers back, 'Since we *don't* know where you are going, how can we know the way?'

I have used his words as the title of this little book, because the essay did not arise out of certainty but out of doubts and questions. 'The Way' was the first name given, in the *Acts of the Apostles* to the Christian religion itself. But nineteen centuries later, we can see that there have been almost as many interpretations of the Way as there have been Christians. Some scholars today would say that it was next to impossible to recover what the historical Jesus was really like; or even to know with certainty what he actually said. Many of the scholars would seem agreed that Jesus was an apocalyptic preacher and healer in a remote province of the Roman Empire who had no intention of founding a Church, still less of setting himself up as 'the Son of God'. So, if there *were* a Way how could we know it?

The second question lying behind this short book is more radical than the first. Even if it is possible (as I believe it is) to recover some picture of what the Christian Way should be, and of what all Christian people have, or should have, in common, how can we know that it is true? The oddness of the story can be lost on those, like me, who have grown fond of it over the years. Wizards arrive from the east and say that they have astrological evidence that a Jewish king has been born. A virgin gives birth to a baby. He is brought up, not in the town where he is alleged to have been born, but in the northern province. He teaches about a Kingdom not of this world in unforgettable, pithy stories and sayings. He heals the sick. He quarrels with the authorities and is put to death in circumstances which students of Jewish and Roman legal procedure find puzzling. He is seen alive three days later by his disciples. By one account, he is seen in Galilee again by some fishermen, achieves an astonishing catch of fish and is then never seen again. In another, he is last seen ascending into the clouds. Twenty years later, his most fervent adherent, a converted Pharisee called Saul or Paul is claiming that within the lifetime of most of his readers, Jesus will return on the clouds and lift them, before their natural death, into the sky. He further preaches that this mysterious judicial murder on Calvary has the power to remove the guilt of all human beings who turn to Christ.

How can we know that any of this is true? On the face of things, it seems pretty improbable. Even if we do not refer to the New Testament writings at all, how can we know that there is a good God? Does the suffering universe suggest any such thing? How can we know anything? So, Thomas asked, How can we know the Way?

It sounds as though he ought to have been given an answer which was intellectually satisfying. Questions which start with the word *How* are requests for explanation. But the answer, startlingly enough, is *I am the Way*. Now, *I am* was the unutterable Holy Name, revealed to Moses from out of the Burning Bush. In placing these syllables on Christ's lips, John is writing theology. But I find it hard to escape the feeling that the sentence has that unmistakable note of puzzling simplicity, the almost maddening quality of a troubling riddle, which characterizes so many of the recorded sayings of Jesus. No one could prove that he actually said it. But nor could anyone prove that he did not. The question begins with the word How. It is answered as if it had begun with the word Who.

I conceived of this essay as an attempt to answer, largely for my own benefit, the question How? How much of the Christian religion, or what survives of it, is really true? How much of the Creed can an honest man still accept? How much is a modern Christian, however attached he is to the old forms and stories, obliged to admit that the atheists have won the argument? If God is all powerful, and His world is in the miserable condition which we can all see, what is the point in continuing to say that God is love?

In the event, however, a bit like the Apostle Thomas, I found myself getting answers which did not seem to be replies to the question I had originally asked, but which made me reconsider the whole matter. If repentance means thinking again, I suppose this essay is an act of repentance. Other people would approach the thing quite differently; I am aware of that. Why write so much about Tolstoy, they would say, and so comparatively little about St Paul? If I reply, like Pontius Pilate, that *What I have written, I have written*, it is not because I think I have penned the last word; still less that I have presented a set of arguments which any unbeliever would find 'unanswerable'. This isn't meant to be that sort of book. It began, long before I thought of writing it, as a series of conversations, and I make no apology for its conversational spirit. As in most conversations the thing is not a logical progression but a series of associated thoughts. At times, there are embarrassing bits. It is embarrassing, talking about God. I have felt it was worth slogging on and trying to ignore the embarrassment.

I start by reconsidering the moral teachings of Jesus. Although I suppose I have heard the Sermon on the Mount, or parts of it, read to me almost hundreds of times, I still feel surprised by it. Is there not something deeply crazy in the notion that we must die in order to live? Even if we thought it was *desirable* to offer no resistance to violence, to take no thought for the morrow, to hoard no wealth, to indulge no carnal appetite, has anyone ever found it to be more than partially possible? And even if we could follow the counsels of perfection spelt out by Jesus, how can we be sure that they were his words?

In its initial form, this essay was not meant to be published. It was simply a way of setting my own thoughts in some sort of order. If I had predicted, at the beginning, how the argument would proceed, I think I would have guessed that in the end, with great regret, I would have echoed Yeats's dismissal of the great Catholic theologian: 'Get you gone, von Hugel, though with blessings on your head!'. The more I dwelt upon the matter, however, the more I discovered that in spite of everything, I did believe the Christian religion to be inescapably and irresistibly true. The writing of the essay became in itself a rediscovery of the Way, the Truth and the Life which, in more thoughtless moods I would have dismissed as unfollowable, unknowable and unlivable. I do not find faith particularly easy and it is with some coyness that I seem to be coming before the public not with a new novel but with 'the old old story' of which the hymn speaks. At the risk of embarrassing everyone, including myself, I offer this un-polished piece of prose to a public who probably shares the various doubts and difficulties I have experienced. I do not think that piety gives us the excuse to shuffle off the hard questions which scholars have posed. And I do not think that we shall ever find the answer to the question in my title on this side of the grave. But nor do I think that our own age has a monopoly of wisdom and it will take more than a handful of textual critics or analytic philosophers to demolish the experience of those millions of men and women who, in all corners of the earth, and for nearly two thousand years, have been able to echo the excited words of the Apostle Andrew: 'We have discovered the Messias (which means the Christ)'.

Those words, incidentally, come from the translation of the Bible by Ronald Knox, which I have used for quotations throughout.

CHAPTER ONE

The Call

Rather less than twenty years ago, when I was a schoolboy, I belonged to a sixth-form society to which we invited visiting speakers. Someone came and told us how the City of London worked. On another week, a politician might come to speak, or a journalist or a writer. One week, a man came and told us about Tolstoy. He spoke, not about Tolstoy's genius as a novelist (which I think I had begun to discover) but about the great act of renunciation which Tolstoy undertook after he had finished *Anna Karenina*. As he spoke, I felt my 'heart burn within me', like the disciples walking to Emmaus after the first Easter. I felt more excited by the story than by any I had ever heard. Here was the greatest genius who had ever written a novel. He was a Russian aristocrat, an ex-soldier, a sensualist, one of the richest characters (in all senses of those words) in the history of literature. And yet, at the very summit of his fame, he wanted to renounce everything, to abandon his estates, his money, the practice of literature, the exercise of his carnal appetites, and to live a life of poverty, like the peasants on his estates. And why? Because he had become convinced that the Sermon preached by Jesus on the mountain towards the beginning of St Matthew's Gospel was simply and literally true.

At the time, I was very young for my fifteen or sixteen years, very impressionable and very enthusiastic. I had already been by turns, a convert to a simple sort of evangelical Christianity; an atheist; a Marxist with particular devotion to the teachings of Chairman Mao. I do not remember in what order I adopted and discarded these enthusiasms. I expect I went through about three or four creeds in each school term. But the Tolstoy thing took hold of me for longer. Strange as it seems to me now, for about two years I tried to practise some of the simpler dictates of the Tolstoyan creed such as vegetarianism. I joined the Peace Pledge Union. I absorbed and re-read as much of his writing as I could. Then, when a few years passed, I found that I had moved on. 'It is the concrete being that reasons,' Newman wrote; 'pass a number of years and I find my mind in a new place. How? The whole man moves, paper logic is but the record of it'. I stumbled on, zig-zagging my way down the road of faith, now believing, now disbelieving, and increasingly concerned with the spiritual journey of Newman himself. Tolstoy was not forgotten. He was put on one side, always haunting my memory.

Lately, for a number of reasons, I have returned to Tolstoy, and once again, I have been overwhelmed by the sheer grandeur and simplicity of his writings on the subject of Christianity. Coming to the story as a grown-up, I am furthermore haunted by his appalling domestic sufferings. Everything about him was great – larger than life – including his faults and his mistakes. How, for instance, could somebody of his extraordinary knowledge of human character have been so *foolish* as to show all his private diaries to his wife? Much of his quest for the Kingdom of God was obscured by his ludicrously Luddite and philistine prejudices. Why, for instance, was it more Christian to travel in a cart than by train? What lunacy can have prompted him to think his own greatest novels (no modesty, here, he was a stranger to modesty) *War and Peace* and *Anna Karenina* were simply *piffle*? How could he have been so arrogant as to dismiss Shakespeare? Oh yes, the faults are all obvious enough to the grown-up reader. And we can read with a lofty cynicism of the great Tolstoy's moral failings. What rows there were at Yasnaya Polyana after he had resolved to put all anger out of his heart! Nor was it necessarily safe for the young peasant girls to get too close to the Count after he had made his notorious vow of complete celibacy.

But Tolstoy himself had an answer which shames any of his detractors:

> "Well, but you, Leo Nikolayevich; you preach – but how about practice?" People always put it to me and always triumphantly shut my mouth with it. You preach, but how do you live? And I reply that I do not preach and cannot preach, though I passionately desire to do so. I could only preach by deeds; and my deeds are bad. What I say is not a sermon, but only a refutation of a false understanding of the Christian teaching and an explanation of its real meaning. Its meaning is not that we should in its name rearrange society by violence: its purpose is to find the meaning of our life in this world. The performance of Christ's five commandments gives that meaning. If you wish to be a Christian, you must fulfil those commands. If you do not wish to fulfil them, don't talk of Christianity. . . . I do not fulfil a ten-thousandth part it is true, and I am to blame for that; but it is not because I do not wish to fulfil them that I fail, but because I do not know how to. Teach me how to escape from the nets of temptation that have ensnared me, help me, and I will fulfil them; but even without help I desire and hope to do so. Blame me – I do that myself – but blame *me*, and not the path I tread, and show to those who ask me where in my opinion the road lies! If I know the road home and go along it drunk, staggering from side to side – does that make the road along which I go a wrong one? . . .

Reading those words again after a gap of nearly twenty years, I was arrested once more by their extraordinary power. They made me read The Sermon on the Mount again, and to see it with fresh eyes. As a young reader of Tolstoy, I was chiefly struck by his failure to live as Jesus said we should. Twenty years later, I am much more astonished by his attempt to do so, than I am by his failure. Most reasonable, decent, Western readers in the latter half of the twentieth century would find the Christ of Saint Matthew's Gospel romantic, but repellent. The brutal paradoxes of the Beatitudes seem inimical to

3

contemporary moral values. Sometimes good agnostics say that they are unable to accept the supernatural elements of the New Testament but that they would like to think that their lives approximate to the values of the Sermon on the Mount. The life of Tolstoy is a vivid illustration of what it would be like if we *truly* wished to live as Jesus taught. The modern, unchristian wisdom, for instance, would consider it impracticable and simply unhealthy to worry about the lustful thoughts which happen to pass through our heart. In the scale of values enunciated by Jesus, 'he who casts his eyes on a woman so as to lust after her has already committed adultery with her in his heart'. (Matthew 5:28). Even if we thought that we *could* prevent ourselves having such thoughts, how many of us believe that we *should*? Certainly many an analyst would be out of business if we truly thought it was possible to banish the very feelings of anger (Matthew 5:22). As for the teachings of Jesus about money and poverty, could anyone who was not, like Tolstoy, a rich aristocrat, contemplate giving up *everything*, and living as the flowers of the field, dependent wholly on the Providence of God? Perhaps a few young men and women nowadays embrace the comparative security of a religious order and believe that they have become poor for Christ's sake. But what of us, who live *in* the world? Do bills pay themselves? Christ told his disciples to pay tax to Caesar, so presumably he did not expect them to be penniless. The renunciation of Tolstoy, when watched from afar, unfolds like a great tragedy, and we can, at this historical distance, be uplifted by its drama. But of *us*: what of us, with our humdrum carnal and economic needs? Surely it would be madness to emulate him, pure insanity to put into practice the self-destructive teachings of Christ.

But, I find that the words of Tolstoy won't be dismissed or ignored. 'If you wish to be a Christian, you must fulfil these commands', he said. And when one turns to the New Testament itself, the paradox of it all becomes even harsher. What would we say of a man who tried to bottle up all his anger, to suppress his sexual nature, who abandoned all earthly security, closed his deposit account and gave the money to the poor?

4

Would we not think that such a person was storing up trouble, behaving in a way which was calculated to produce a total personal collapse? Jesus says this about such a man:

> Whoever, then, hears these commandments of mine and carries them out, is like a wise man who built his house upon rock; and the rain fell and the floods came and the winds blew and beat upon that house, but it did not fall; it was founded upon rock. But whoever hears these commandments of mine and does not carry them out is like a fool, who built his house upon sand; and the rain fell and the floods came and the winds blew and beat upon that house, and it fell; and great was the fall of it.

> (Matthew 7:24–28)

These words at the end of the Sermon on the Mount are perhaps the most shocking and preposterous of all. For, whatever else Christ appears to offer in his manifesto for the Kingdom, it is not rock-like security. From the very opening words, *Blessed are the poor in spirit*, the paradox is with us. *Blessed are the poor in spirit* does not mean the same, precisely, as blessed are the poor. And it is conspicuous that those who are professionally engaged in teaching the truth of the Incarnation, the clergy, should have spent so much of their energy over the years in denying the truth of these words, *Blessed are the poor in spirit*, the very first words uttered, in St Matthew's Sermon, by the Incarnate God. We have been told that there is such a thing as 'evangelical poverty' which is is somehow different from real poverty, or that the words mean, 'Blessed are the needy': that is, Blessed are those who recognise their need for God's grace. But this Beatitude, *Blessed are the poor in spirit* is really no more than an introduction to the other sayings of Christ in the same Sermon.

> Do not lay up treasure for yourselves on earth, where there is moth and rust to consume it, where there are thieves to break in and steal it; lay up treasure for yourselves in heaven.

5

. . . A man cannot be the slave of two masters at once; either he will hate the one and love the other, or he will devote himself to the one and despise the other. You must serve God or money; you cannot serve both.

(Matthew 6:19–20, 24)

And there is abundant evidence in the Gospels that Jesus believed that 'it is easier for a camel to pass through a needle's eye, than for a man to enter the kingdom of heaven when he is rich'. (Matthew 19:24). One can reserve for the moment the casuist's discussion of 'how poor is poor', or the common-sense notion that we have 'got to live' and provide for the future, the children, and old age. Christ specifically tells his disciples not to do those things. He says that we should take no thought for the morrow (Matthew 6:34) and not worry about how we are to be clothed or fed. (Matthew 6:28)

'The poor have the good news preached to them' (Matthew 11:5). It came as the climax of his message to John the Baptist in prison. It seems from its rhetorical placing in that sentence to be more important, in Christ's scale of values, than the blind seeing, or the lame walking, or the lepers being made clean; more important, or more miraculous. So indeed it is. The great Christian miracle for St Paul was that God dispossessed himself and became like a poor slave in order to teach the human race the way of dispossession. (Philippians 2:7)

But in common-sense terms, we know that the poor *aren't* blessed. What is blessed about the filth of shanty-towns? What is blessed about a disease-ridden African village full of starving children? What can the poor in such places hope for, live for? We suffer in the West from the deadening effects of material-ism. But we can at least see that wealth, rightly used, has enabled us to lift ourselves above the purely material level of the beasts. Shakespeare was patronised by a rich man, the Earl of Southampton. Michelangelo painted his masterpieces at the behest of rich popes. The sublime masses and symphonies of Haydn were paid for. The great Gothic cathedrals, the swoop-ing, well-planted parks of eighteenth century noblemen, the

6

great canvases of Tintoretto or Rembrandt were all produced by money, and they would not have existed if everyone in Christian Europe had followed purely the dictates of the Christian religion.

There is nothing bland about the Beatitudes. They are all hard: hard in the sense of flinty – as the final metaphor of the Sermon would suggest; hard in the sense of difficult; hard, even, in the sense of merciless. For the fifth beatitude, *Blessed are the merciful* sounds easy enough until Christ expounds it. We are not merely to show mercy comparatively in the manner of a magistrate reducing a poacher's sentence from hanging to penal servitude. Mercy in the moral universe of the Sermon seems to demand total open-heartedness.

> You have heard that it was said, An eye for an eye and a tooth for a tooth. But I tell you that you should not offer resistance to injury; if a man strikes thee on thy right cheek, turn the other cheek also towards him; if he is ready to go to law with thee over thy coat, let him have it and thy cloak with it;

> (Matthew 5:38–41)

One feature of the debate about nuclear weapons which goes on at the moment, is how vociferously certain church-leaders have returned to the Christian pacifism of the Sermon on the Mount. It would seem (though papal utterances are always hard to disentangle) as though the Pope had now discarded the old notion of a 'just war'. Many churchmen seem to say that they object to nuclear weapons but they do not object to 'conventional warfare', by which they presumably mean things like the Battle of the Somme and the bombing of Dresden. Others have casuistically, and perhaps wisely, argued that Our Lord's Sermon on the Mount was not directed to nations but to *individuals*. But how does that alter the morality of the case? It is an individual and not a nation who pulls the trigger, or presses the button. The pacifism of Christ was obviously absolute. It was not of a 'militant' kind.

7

He did not hurl abuse at centurions. On the contrary, he conversed with them; one of them, he regarded as being a man of greater faith than his own fellow-Israelites (Matthew 8:10). It is also true that he told his disciples that they should not set themselves up as judges of other people (Matthew 7:1). But if it is true that St Matthew's Gospel does not anticipate the moral complexities of the nuclear debate, there can be no escaping its absolute rejection of reprisal as a moral principle. If a society were ordered along the lines of the Sermon, it would be necessary not merely to abolish the armed forces, but also the police and the law-courts. In social terms, it is a recipe for anarchy. In personal terms, it is loudly and inescapably obvious that Our Lord forbade his followers to defend themselves against attack, just as he forbade them to provide for the future by saving up money.

Then again, in the sixth beatitude, Jesus says *Blessed are the clean of heart*. 'In Hebrew psychology, the heart is the seat of thought and will rather than of emotion', says one modern commentary on this verse. If that is so, it means that Jesus makes a greater, not a lesser demand. We could all get into a *mood* of piety if we wanted to, in which we felt, or persuaded ourselves that we felt, as pure as driven snow. It is much less easy to control the movement of the mind. It is harder yet to purify the will. If by *heart* is really meant the whole inner man, his affections, his prejudices, his habits of mind, his emotional history, all that we mean by his *character*, these things are to a large degree unchangeable. By the time that our 'characters are formed', there is very little we can do about them. We can resolve to do better; we can undertake a major programme of reform. But all the scars and shapes of our old existence will still be there.

Common sense rebels against the call to poverty. (It rebels in vain, but it rebels.) In this saying, by contrast, the human heart itself is reproached by Christ. It shows that his standards are meant to be impossibly high. In the course of the Sermon, he says (scholars tell us that the author of St Matthew's Gospel makes him say) that he does not want to overthrow the old Judaic law. Whether or not that verse has been invented by an early Jewish Christian anxious not to lose contact with the practices of his old faith, we cannot escape the searching perfectionism of what follows. The old law had said that it was wrong to commit murder.

> But I tell you that any man who is angry with his brother must answer for it before the court of justice, and any man who says Raca to his brother must answer for it before the Council; and any man who says to his brother, Thou fool, must answer for it in Hell fire.

> (Matthew 5:22–23)

For someone like myself who is not merely congenitally irascible, but also professionally committed, as a journalist, to commenting upon human folly, this is perhaps the most disturbing passage in the entire sermon. In his story of Dives and Lazarus, Jesus tells us that the rich man, who ignored his warning to embrace holy poverty, was sent to hell. (Luke 16:22). Likewise, in the sermon on the Mount, he implies that hell is the reward of those who commit the sins of the flesh.

> If thy right eye is the occasion of thy falling into sin, pluck it out and cast it away from thee; better to lose one part of thy body than to have the whole cast into hell.

> (Matthew 5:29)

And, more generally,

> It is a broad gate and a wide road that leads on to perdition.

> (Matthew 7:13)

It is the narrow way which leads on to salvation. It is the chaste, meek-hearted pacifist with no money in the world who builds his house on a rock. It is the libidinous, aggressive man, storing up quantities of this world's riches, who is building his house on the sand.

9

When I contemplate the lives of other people, I am just about prepared to concede the romantic appeal of all this. Sitting on a commuter train, perhaps, and watching everyone going to work, I see the lecherous business-men, giving themselves ulcers by overwork, their minds perpetually engaged, even when at home, by the threats of auditors and the hopes of foreign contracts, changes in interest rates and all the arcane movements and mysteries of money. I compare their worried, pampered faces with the quiet serenity that I have seen on the faces of monks who – mad by the standards of the world – have abandoned the hope of riches and the gratifications of the flesh. I think of promiscuous young women I know, their young faces already raddled with late nights, messy love affairs and too much dope and drink, and compare them with the radiant calm of some of the Christian women I know. In such reveries, the Sermon on the Mount, with all its apparent reversal of common sense, seems luminously sane.

But, to tell the truth, only momentarily so. For the Sermon very specifically tells us not to judge other people. It is not addressed to the others. It is addressed to me. And this explains, perhaps, its abiding power over the centuries. I know with perfect certainty that I have not lived my life according to the dictates of this Sermon. The example of the great Tolstoy would seem to suggest that these counsels of perfection could not even be attempted without failure. But as soon as the words of Christ shine like a spotlight on one's own condition, rather than on the lives of others, their effect is different. It may well be the case that I have not tried to practise Christianity, but I am not certain that life has been any the better for that omission. Here I am, stuck in my mid-thirties with the responsibilities of earning a living and providing for a family. It should be very easy to shrug and say that I have no intention of plunging my children into poverty or adopting the Simple Life. But Christ's words do not go away as easily as that. Nor do I think it is simply because I have heard them since childhood and formed a sentimental attachment to them, while doing next to nothing to put them into practice.

Why is it that, the older one grows, the more topsy-turvy

the wisdom of Christ appears; and yet the more it appears to be wisdom? He seems to be looking at life upside down; he tells us that the poor have security, the mourners will be happy, the sexually deprived will be the most fulfilled. It seems, by the wisdom of this world, as if he got everything the wrong way round. But live a bit, and one discovers that this is not necessarily the case at all. If the world itself is inverted, then the only way to see it clearly is upside down. If the values of the world are the wrong way round, then the only way to wisdom is to stand those values on their head. When we say that we lose the idealism of our youth, we often add that moral choice becomes more complicated with age. We speak as if complexity were a good thing and as though moral sight, like eyesight, got better with age. But some of us could see more clearly when we were sixteen than when we are sixty. I remember something about accepting the Kingdom as a little child. And I remember my first excitement at Tolstoy's words, 'If you wish to be a Christian, you must fulfil these commands. If you do not wish to fulfil them, don't talk of Christianity'. The words won't go away. Jesus said, 'Heaven and earth shall pass away, but my words shall not pass away'.

CHAPTER TWO

The Way

'If you don't wish to fulfil them, don't talk of Christianity', Tolstoy said, speaking of the words of the Sermon on the Mount. And, considering that they offer, as far as I can make out, an unattainable counsel of perfection, why do I not just abandon the whole thing? The counsels of perfection, as well as being impossible, are calculated to make me unhappy. Jesus himself says as much in the beatitudes when he promises that his 'blessed ones' will be the poor, the meek, the mournful and those who are persecuted. It would only be worth enduring all this discomfort and unhappiness, surely, if the supernatural elements in the Gospel were true.

This is something which, over the years, has come to puzzle me about Tolstoy. After his initial conversion to Christianity, he appeared to accept all the teachings of the Orthodox church. But when he decided that the rites and ceremonies of that church were ridiculous, it was not long before he had come to the belief that most of the supernatural stories in the Gospels were make-believe. It is not really clear, for instance, whether he believed in the Resurrection. But the more he discarded the supernatural elements of his faith, the more urgently he advocated the moral excellence of the Sermon on the Mount. 'The essence of Christianity is the fulfilment of the will of God'.

How unlike the sort of Christianity I have intermittently tried to follow over the years since I abandoned my Tolstoyan phase! Not long after that, I embraced Catholicism, first of the Anglo- and then of the Roman variety. It might be thought that the intellectual demands of Catholicism are greater than the simple requirements of Tolstoyanism. But this is not the case. The sort of Catholicism which attracted me was that propounded by such figures as Hilaire Belloc, for whom 'the Christian religion . . . was a thing, not a theory. It was expressed in what I have called an organism, and that organism was the Catholic Church'. He imagines a dinner party in Carthage in AD 225 in which the guests are all discussing religion. One of the guests expresses admiration for the Christian literature and says, 'For my part I have come to make it a sort of rule to act as this Man Christ would have had me act. He seems to me to have led the most perfect life I ever read of, and the practical maxims which are attached to His Name seem to me a sufficient guide to life. That', he will conclude simply, 'is the groove into which I have fallen, and I do not think I shall ever leave it'. Let us call the man who has so spoken Ferreolus. Would Ferreolus have been a *Christian*? Would the officials of the Roman Empire have called him a *Christian*? Would he have been in danger of unpopularity where *Christians* were unpopular? Would *Christians* have received him among themselves as part of their strict and still somewhat secret society? Would he have counted with any single man of the whole empire as one of the *Christian* body? The answer is most emphatically *No*.

Tolstoy by this definition would evidently not have been a Christian. Belloc's belief was that Christ founded the Church and that, forever after, the Church spoke and acted for Him on earth. The Gospels themselves are products of the Church. If we merely accept, therefore, that Christ founded the Church and that we ought to belong to it, all the other theological truths with claims on our acceptance fall into place. We do not worry if *we* find it difficult to accept the Resurrection, the Ascension, or the Assumption of the Blessed Virgin as things which literally took place in the realm of nature. All we need to do is to assent to these things as the teachings of the Catholic Church. I have been engaged for the last few years in writing the biography of Belloc – a great man, though not so great a man as Tolstoy – and I can now see that this attitude to

Catholicism is really the last refuge of scepticism. 'I am by all my nature of mind sceptical', he wrote to his friend G. K. Chesterton when Chesterton too embraced the Roman obedience. 'I am alone and unfed, the more do I affirm the Sanctity, the Unity, the Infallibility of the Catholic Church . . .'

My sojourn in the Church of Rome was as brief as my flirtation with Tolstoyanism. When, at the age of 20, I married a member of the Church of England who did not wish to make the promises then necessary before marrying a Catholic, I switched my allegiance back to the English Church. I never was officially 'received into' the Church of England, so I suppose that by some canons my official status is that of a 'lapsed Catholic'. But I retained for many years Belloc's way of looking at the Christian faith. In many respects, it is so historically true. We would not have the New Testament were it not for the Early Church. It is the Church, 'the blessed company of all faithful people', as the Prayer Book calls it, which has preserved the records of Christ for us into our own age.

I do not want to enter immediately into the question of whether the Church of Rome is the One True Church, or whether the Catholic Church is a thing of many branches, of which the Church of England is one, or whether Christ is present anywhere where two or three are gathered together in his name. I can only record that after many years of professing a stout sort of Catholic orthodoxy, and scoffing at the idiotic utterances of modernist clergymen, I found, imperceptibly, that the ground had shifted under my feet. I attributed it to the foolish passion for change which appeared to have overtaken both the Church of Rome and the Church of England. Nothing would stay the same. Formerly beautiful churches were suddenly wrecked by having ugly new nave altars installed. The matchless old liturgies were ditched in favour of rites whose banality I found a source of embarrassment. Moreover, it was very hard to know whether any of the old orthodoxies which the Church was supposed to enshrine really were believed by the majority of the faithful.

At the Roman church near where I live, for instance, did the jolly folksy Mass, at which children were not discouraged from haring round the altar during the consecration, and at which the laity were bidden to come and help themselves from the brimming chalices on the holy table – did all this suggest an awe-struck belief in the real presence of Christ in the Eucharist? Did the matier overtures of the 'ecumenists', who appeared happy to discard articles of faith for which martyrs, on both sides, had been prepared to die, suggest a devotion to Truth or a complete intellectual vacuity? The theologians (I spent a year at the university reading theology) seemed to take it as axiomatic that such doctrines as the Virgin Birth were pious fables, and many of them only had the haziest belief in the Resurrection. Only faintly lunatic Christians appeared to retain a belief in Hell.

Through all this familiar turmoil of mid-twentieth century Christianity it was easy enough to go on blaming 'the Church' for having changed, and to get angry at the uninspired new liturgies and translations of the bible. I still think there is every cause for anger at many of the vandalistic reforms which have been thrust upon the unwilling 'faithful'. But underneath the bluff Bellocian attitudes which I might on occasion affect, I knew that I was quietly sinking into agnosticism. When 'the Church', in a rock-like way 'stood firm' in the matter of doctrine, it was possible to sustain a measure of agnosticism. You accepted 'the Faith' as a 'Thing'. 'I was never made for understanding this "union with God" business', Belloc said on one occasion and, on another, that he had no devotion to the person of Christ, and only accepted His divinity because the Church told him to do so.

But, hold on! Why do you accept what the Church tells you? Because you believe it to have been founded by Christ. The argument appears to have come in a crazy circle in which 'the Church', the 'Thing', 'It' is more important than the Person who was alleged to have founded It.

If I had kept up a faithful practice of interior prayer, I do not doubt that I would have weathered these storms. As it was, I prayed less and less, and with an increasing sense when I did so that I was indulging in nonsense. In such a 'dessicate' state of mind, I could then begin to ask myself alarmingly direct questions. I still went to church. I still luxuriated, when it could be found, in the reassuring old words of the Book of Common Prayer. But, during the sermon, I would take to flicking through my Prayer Book and reading the Thirty-Nine articles.

IV. *Of the Resurrection of Christ*
Christ did truly rise again from death, and took again his body, with flesh, bones and all things appertaining to the perfection of Man's nature; wherewith he ascended into Heaven, and there sitteth, until he return to judge all Men at the last day.

I wonder how many Western Christians today truly believe this. Modern Christians spoke a lot about 'the Resurrection experience'. It was the experience of the Risen Christ which, for them, created the Church and continued to sustain it. An attractively nebulous concept in many ways. But . . . 'flesh, bones and all things pertaining to the perfection of Man's nature; wherewith he ascended into Heaven'.

How easy it was to pour scorn on the poor old 'Bishop of Woolwich' as, to my generation, the author of *Honest to God* will always be. He had shocked everyone in the 1960s by saying that God was not 'up there'; to which his fellow-bishops, after a little ruffled expression of disapproval, replied that, even if He wasn't, He was 'in here' or 'out there somewhere'. But the 'up' question is not altogether absurd. After all, St Luke, who told the story of the Ascension in the first place, had a completely different picture of the cosmos from our own. *We* know that if a human being were launched from a hillside in Galilee he could go on into space indefinitely before he reached 'Heaven'. But if Our Lord did not rise into the air with flesh, bones and the rest, what happened to him? Is the resurrection of the flesh, after all, a mere metaphor? And if it is, was not St Paul right when he wrote to the Corinthians: 'If the dead do not rise, then Christ has not risen either; and if

Christ has not risen, then our preaching is groundless, and your faith, too, is groundless'. (I Corinthians 15:13)

How easily, in the end, the house of cards collapses. It was only when it had done so, that I began to realise that it was years since I had thought about *Jesus*. I had talked about churches which did or did not contain 'Our Lord', by which I meant His sacramental presence, reserved in a beautifully veiled tabernacle. I had prayed to His Sacred Heart. I had been moved, as I always have been, always will be, by the Eucharistic hymns. For some reason, thinking about Jesus had formed no part of my piety. Many people I know, Christian and non-Christian, spend a lot of time trying to imagine what he was like. I remember once overhearing a Protestant Irish nurse telling some children what sort of toys the Baby Jesus played with in his bath. I have heard many sermons which were hardly less fanciful. In fact, we actually *know* almost nothing about Jesus as an historical character. I once heard a professor of theology ridiculously enunciate the view that the only thing we knew about the Founder of the Christian religion was that he had a verbal mannerism: *verily verily I say unto you*. This was too idiosyncratic, the professor thought, to have been worth inventing.

Other professors of theology have not been so sceptical, but taken as a whole, modern New Testament scholarship does not leave us with a very rounded picture of Our Lord. Place of birth? Dubious. Many consider the Bethlehem infancy narratives were invented to tie in with the prophecies of Micah about 'thou, Bethlehem in the land of Judah art not the least among the princes of Judah'. Profession? Dubious. We are told that the old Aramaic word meaning carpenter or craftsman (*naggar*) is often used in Talmudic sayings to mean a scholar or a learned man. So, out goes the stable at Bethlehem, the carpenter's shop at Nazareth and, for all we can really know anything about them, Mary and Joseph too. Most of the professors seem to be happy with believing that Jesus emanated from Nazareth in Galilee. Most would agree that he was an itinerant exorcist and healer, though they would all differ in the extent to which they believe his miracle-cures were *authen-*

tic. They rightly point out that we are not told any of the biographical details which would be usual in a modern chronicle: Jesus's marital status, for instance, or his physical appearance.

The extent of Christ's difference from other Jewish teachers of his day, the reasons for his clashes with the Pharisees, and the details of how he was finally rounded up and put on trial all seem to be matters over which the scholars disagree. Many appear to doubt that he was put on trial in any formal sense. All seem agreed (except for a few cranky theorists) that he was put to death by Crucifixion and that he died and was buried. Almost every New Testament scholar clings superstitiously to the notion that the oldest of the gospels is that of Mark. They point out that Mark's gospel ends simply with the women coming to the tomb, finding the stone rolled away, and 'a young man seated, and they were afraid'. (Mark 16:5. The continuation of this chapter is generally agreed to be a later interpolation.)

The empty tomb may remain to baffle us. But that is as far as scholarship, in its cautious way, is prepared to go. That is as far as I went, I suppose, when I read theology ten years ago. And since so little can be known, surely it is only sensible to admit that we are agnostic, to admit that a very large number of Christian people have been deluded in their belief by the pious fables and traditions and accretions which superstition has added to the bare details of historical evidence.

I think in a quiet way, this had been my position for a number of years, though, quite illogically, I had kept on going to church, sometimes in a Tennysonian mood of faintly trusting the larger hope, sometimes for reasons of personal nostalgia too deep for me to analyse, sometimes out of mere habit; but never wholly for those reasons. Something drew me back. I was in the position of thinking that even if it was all untrue, it was so firmly embedded in my system that I would never escape it.

But that nebulous acceptance of Christianity as something as it were in the blood is not enough to explain the impact of re-reading the Sermon on the Mount, and for that matter the

Gospels as a whole. It is ridiculous to say that we know nothing of Jesus, merely because we cannot picture what he was like physically, merely because the evangelists have not left us a lot of gossipy anecdotes about the carpenter's (or scholar's – what was a scholar doing in Nazareth?) house in Galilee, or merely because we happen to know more about cosmology than St Luke.

'Whereupon Jesus said to the Twelve, Would you, too, go away? Simon Peter answered him, Lord to whom should we go? Thy words are the words of eternal life;' (John 6:69). It is the words of Jesus which compel our attention, and it is in his words that we initially meet him. The New Testament commentaries abound in references to the Old Testament, to the Jewish Apocrypha, to the Dead Sea Scrolls, to Philo, designed to show us how much Jesus had in common with his antecedents and his contemporaries. It would be very surprising if he did not have *something* in common with the tradition and setting from which he sprang. But it would be a denial of history, a denial of the experience of countless men and women throughout the centuries, if one thought that *all* the sayings of Jesus were little more than a first century semitic pot-pourri. They are blindingly and terrifyingly different from anything that anyone has ever said before or since: in their absolutism, and, at first sight, in their mercilessness. G. K. Chesterton, in *The Everlasting Man*, remarks that the Christ of the Gospels 'might seem actually more strange and terrible than the Christ of the Church'. This is surely a just description of One who could tell human beings that their most blessed condition was one of abject poverty; of one who recommended, in a doubtless metaphorical sense, that if our hand offends us we should cut it off; of one who terrified the demons in the Gerasene lunatics and sent the herd of pigs screaming over the cliff; of one who promised his disciples that they would be 'hated by all men because you bear my name'; of one who said that he came to bring a sword, not peace:

I have come to set a man at variance with his father, and the daughter with her mother, and the daughter-in-law with her mother-in-law; a man's enemies will be the people of his own house. He is not worthy of me, that loves father or mother more; he is not worthy of me, that loves son or daughter more; he is not worthy of me that does not take up his cross and follow me. He who secures his own life will lose it; it is the man who loses his life for my sake that will secure it.

(Matthew 10:35–40)

We can say a lot about the man who said those words. But what we can't say is that *we do not know anything about him*. What does it matter whether he was tall or short or fat or thin or married or unmarried or a carpenter or a rabbi? The words shout at you. If an individual saying or *logion* finds its parallel in some other place, the effect of the whole collection of sayings is unmistakable. His words stand all our ordinary worldly standards of common sense on their heads. We can characterise almost all his utterances as being of this essentially paradoxical kind. If we wish to gain life, we must lose it. If we wish to lay up treasure in heaven, we must be poor. However the various redactors or evangelists have arranged the sayings, and whatever the difficulty of understanding how individual sayings apply, the manifesto for the Kingdom is unmistakably disturbing. The words which are attributed to him by all the Gospel-writers proclaim him as a figure wholly at variance with the wisdom of this world. 'My kingdom does not belong to this world', Saint John has him saying to Pilate, when the whole conflict has reached its climax.

In John's Gospel this conflict of Jesus with the values of this world is more clearly marked even than in the other three Gospels. He tells Nicodemus that no one can see the kingdom without being born anew (John 3:4). To his enemies, he says that it is because they do not belong to God that they will not heed his words (John 8:47). To his disciples, he says that if they have any love of him they must keep his commandments (John 14:15). And he warns them that if they *do* keep his commandments, they will experience the same harsh reaction as he experiences himself.

If the world hates you, be sure that it hated me before it learned to hate you. If you belonged to the world, the world would know you for its own and love you; it is because you do not belong to the world, because I have singled you out from the midst of the world, that the world hates you.

(John 15:18–20)

*

I can not pretend to find these sayings congenial; nor even, in any obvious way *attractive*. They are obviously the opposite of attractive, and we might ask the question, if Jesus was not divine, why need we take any notice of them? Put as a reply to St John 14:15 we might say, since we do not love Jesus, why should we keep his commandments? But this is really to argue from an absurd set of assumptions. It assumes that we 'know' or 'think' that Jesus was or was not divine. But what are those assumptions based on? Belloc and his like would say that they were based entirely on Church doctrine. But this, which sounds like a satisfactory argument, is really an evasive one. For, what is the Church doctrine based on?

It is based on a number of things which I do not want to discuss now: the peculiarly esoteric theological arguments of the Council of Nicaea, the collective experience of Christianity around the Eucharistic altar, the charismatic phenomenon of Christians who had 'received Jesus into their hearts' or some similar experience; the 'historical evidence' in the Gospels – the empty tomb, the stories of Jesus's reappearances after his death, and so forth. It is perfectly possible to imagine Christianity having flourished with all these elements and yet to lack its distinctive colouring were it not for the *words of Jesus*. I can quite see that Creed, Eucharist, Personal experience, and Historical evidence are all essential ingredients in a definition of Christianity. But would we feel the strange mixture of attraction and repulsion for the Christian religion if all the words of Jesus had been the opposite of what they in fact were? Let us suppose that the historical evidence for the resurrection is so indisputable that no rational person could dispute it. Let us assume, even more fantastically, that the Creeds are completely comprehensible and that we believe that the 'winning side' in any one of the early councils of the Church was always guided by the Holy Spirit of God. Let us assume that we have had a living experience of the Resurrected Jesus, an experience which we shared with an undivided Christendom around the altar Sunday by Sunday. Let us suppose all these fantastic things. Would the religion of Christ compel our allegiance if, when we read the Gospels, we found that he had been an advocate of aggression, cruelty, greed and lust? If the Beatitudes were deprived of all paradox and became a mere analysis of what actually happens in the world, would we be interested in them? Blessed are the rich. It is the powerful who inherit the earth. There is no comfort for those who mourn, but since there is no comfort for those who remain and 'you can't take it with you' you might as well drown your sorrows in alcohol and rich living? . . .

Would a God who spoke these words compel our attention? On the contrary, we would know him not to have been God. It is in the maddeningly *contrary* quality of the words of Jesus that we know him to have spoken the word of God. The words will not be ignored. They can not be absorbed into 'theology' or a view of the Church. The divinity of Jesus, if we believe in it at all, can only be accepted if we are prepared to 'keep his commandments'. This is reiterated in each of the Gospels over and over again. In other words, whatever *other* grounds we might find for believing in the divinity of Christ, we must find his divinity in his words. We do not 'accept' the words 'because' he was divine. We are drawn to the words, as to the words of divinity.

The words are quite as stern, and they are much more demanding, than any that were uttered to Moses on Mount Sinai. It is comforting to a sceptical modern mind like my own to re-read the story of how Moses received the Law. After Moses had been communing for a long time on the mountain, the people down below persuaded Aaron to create for them their own false religion, the worship of the Golden Calf. So has it been ever since, for false religions are much easier to control than true ones. Instead of contemplating the truth of God's word, all you have to worry about is whether you are keeping the rules of your particular church. And, if that gets boring, you can easily become absorbed in the life-consuming hobby of tinkering with those rules. When I visited the General Synod of the Church of England, and saw the corridors swarming with bishops and parsons all busily discussing the management of their own affairs (should they ordain women, should they include this or that rite in their new service book, is Synod working 'effectively' etc., etc.), I felt it was appropriate that their (extremely good) restaurant was called the Golden Calf. But truly religious men, both in churches and out of them, are always called to commune *alone* with God; and, having no taste at all for the worship of Golden Calves, they strain after the vision of God.

> Give me then, said Moses, the sight of thy glory. And he answered, All my splendour shall pass before thy eyes, and I will pronounce, in thy presence, my own divine name, the name of the Lord who shews favour where he will, grants pardon where he will. But, my face, he said, thou canst not see; mortal man cannot see me, and live to tell of it. Then he said, There is a place here, close by me, where thou mayst stand on a rock; there I will station thee in a cleft of the rock, while my glory passes by, and cover thee with my right hand until I have gone past. So when I take my hand away, thou shalt follow me with thy eyes, but my face thou canst not see.
>
> (Exodus 33:18–23)

The true God has gone on eluding the sight of men ever since, though those, like Moses, who have even glimpsed the reflexion of his glory often *shine* with the experience. In fact, when I return to the Bible and re-read it, I have been struck by this common theme linking the Old and the New Testaments. In both cases, God is firmly and definitely invisible to mortal eyes. No man, St John says (John 1:18), has ever seen God. In the Old Testament, first through the Law of Moses, and then through the utterances of the various prophets, there is reiterated the notion that we can only know God by serving him; we can only serve him by following his will and 'walking in the way of his commandments'.

To that extent, whether we regard St Matthew's Gospel as an authentic witness to the historical Jesus, or whether we regard it as a collection of Jesus's sayings rearranged by a conscious 'Judaiser', we can still see that Jesus is recognisably a Jewish teacher.

'How remarkable the Jews are', a convert from that race to Roman Catholicism once said to me. 'They have gone on believing for years and years and years in a God you can't *see*. With us it's easy. You know what the Sacred Heart is like, you can go into church and see a statue of it. But the Jews have to believe without seeing'. Very true. 'The wind breathes where it will', said Jesus the Jew, 'and thou canst hear the sound of it, but knowest nothing of the way it came or the way it goes'; and again, 'the time is coming, nay, has already come, when true worshippers will worship the Father in spirit and in truth; such men as these the Father claims for his worshippers'. (John 3:8, John 4:23).

Those who say that Christianity is something much more than a moral code are perfectly right. One frequently hears it affirmed, even, that it has nothing to do with morality; further, that it is amoral, or immoral. But if that is true of certain *interpretations of* Christianity, it cannot be said to be true of the words of Christ. You may find them, as I do, frequently troubling, frightening, over-demanding. You cannot escape them. We must face them and then reject or accept them as we will. St John's Gospel, often thought to be anti-Jewish, takes almost the same line as St Matthew's. The judgment, as with the fate of the men building their houses on rock or on sand, depends upon the degree to which you accept Christ's *words*. 'The man who makes me of no account, and does not accept my words, has a judge appointed to try him; it is the message I have uttered that will be his judge at the last day' (John 12:48).

It brings us back to Tolstoy. Admittedly, by the time he

wrote his religious treatises, he had a bee in his bonnet about the wickedness of the Russian Orthodox Church (who had excommunicated him) and he had become violently anti-sacramental, anti-mystical, anti-salvationist in his understanding of the Gospel. But if for the moment one discounts that, how can one answer the simplicity of his claim that,

> The Christian teaching seems to make life impossible only when people mistake the indication of an ideal for the laying down of a rule. Only then do the principles presented by Christ's teaching appear to make life impossible. In reality those principles alone make true life possible and without them it cannot exist.
>
> "Too much should not be demanded", people usually say when discussing the requirements of the Christian teaching. "It is an impossible demand that we should not take any care for the future, as is said in the Gospel – though one should not be too careful about it. It won't do to give away everything to the poor, but one should give a certain definite part. It is not necessary to strive after chastity, but one should avoid debauchery. One need not leave wife and children, but should not have too great a partiality for them", and so on.

One must recognise that Tolstoy is right. This *is* what the majority of Christians say when confronted with the Sermon on the Mount. One has heard such compromises of it from pulpits on innumerable occasions. If I am right in imagining that it is in the words of Christ that one is first confronted by his divinity, there is more danger to religion in compromising the Sermon on the Mount than there is in doubting the miraculous details of the Resurrection, the Ascension, and so forth. For if we are to love him we are to keep his commandments. And if we do not keep his words and commandments we shall be like the fool who built his house on the sand.

For Tolstoy, Christ's teaching resolved itself into five ideals after which we ought to aspire. First, the ideal of universal love, and of banishing ill-will for anyone. The second is the ideal of perfect chastity. The third is the ideal of living in the present and not caring for the future. The fourth is never to use violence and the fifth is to love our enemies. Under all these heads, the various specific injunctions of Christ – such as not to lay up treasure – may be gathered.

Tolstoy wrote just before the First World War. The seventy years which have elapsed since then do not suggest that the world has taken any of his warnings to heart. But the less the world takes them to heart, the more urgently sane the words seem. The Jesus of St John's Gospel, talking by night with Nicodemus, said that he had not come into the world to reject it or to judge it. What happened was the opposite. It was the world who rejected the values of God. 'Rejection lies in this, that when the light came into the world men preferred darkness to light; preferred it because their doings were evil' (John 3:19). The effects of this judgement or rejection unfold with more exaggerated ugliness in each generation. Perhaps the world is no more violent now than it was seventy years ago, but it is unquestionably more dangerous, for we have managed to invent infinitely destructive channels of our violence. Perhaps (though I rather doubt this) we are no more unchaste than our great-grandparents or grandparents. Certainly there is no abundant evidence that the so-called Sexual Revolution has ushered in a dawn of widespread contentment. As for the Christian ideal that we should not set our heart on the riches of this world, does that seem any more crazy than the universal materialism with which one is surrounded – successive Governments boring us with their inability to control interest figures and money supply; banks luring us all to pay on credit for things we don't want; half the world wallowing in food they would prefer to throw away rather than sell cheap, the other half dying of starvation.

These features of life have become so familiar to us that we have become used to them, just as the familiar Christian cries of horror at the evils of the twentieth century have become so embedded in cliché and clap-trap that we take even those for granted. Christians have much to answer for in so far as they are not only very frequently boring themselves, but they allow the most boring of their number to be elevated to positions of authority in the churches. The message therefore is dulled, and swallowed up by the ordinary common-sense concerns of living, like the seeds in Jesus's story of the Sower. (Matthew 13:1–23). It really is possible to live in our mad world and forget how mad it is. And it is possible for the Christian message to come at us so muffled by the obsessions of the clergy about the Brandt report or the CND or the Festival of Light that its individually arresting quality becomes muddled and blunted.

That is why I find the rediscovery of Tolstoy so shocking, and so illuminating. I find myself now turning over photographs of him and looking at him, almost as the faithful in his own land, much to his scorn, worshipped holy ikons. There is only peace in the last photograph of all when he lies dead on his pillow at Astapovo railway station. Until that moment, in almost every photograph (and there are many) his vast dome of a forehead is knit with anger, and his eyes stare wildly, darkly on either side of the thick, almost negroid nose. He looks never more desperate than when placed beside his unfortunate harridan of a wife, a woman who was so selfish and egotistic that she did not even begin to understand the high seriousness of his quest, his pilgrimage.

By his firm reiteration of the ethics of Christ, Tolstoy made his own life a sort of parable for the twentieth century. In that sense, he was its greatest prophet. If one tries to assess his religious importance, one should not look merely at the numerous hangers-on, the vegetarian crack-pots, the anarchists – nor even, though they remain his most devoted admirers, the many peasants in the regions of Yasnaya Polyana who, to this day, revere him. More than any other writer, Tolstoy rescued Christ from the deadening clutch of the clergy and gave him back to the world. He rescued above all the words of Christ, the inescapable notion in the Gospels that if we would be the disciples of Jesus, we must keep his commandments. And he was able to show to the world the practical consequences of not keeping what he called the five commandments of Christ.

But at the same time, though it has to be said that he achieved more in his heroic renunciations than most of us would be able to do, he was unable to address himself to the practical tensions caused between the height of Christ's ideal, and the tug of the world, the flesh and the devil. As it happened, the Tolstoyan communities which tried to live by his ideals all fizzled out, for one reason or another. But even if they had not done so, is that the way that Jesus really meant the human race to live? The question prompts the reply that he did not think about the human race, that he hardly thought beyond Galilee, and certainly not beyond the Jewish race. (There is some evidence for this. A Jewish scholar reminds us, 'not only did he feel himself sent to the Jews alone; he qualified non-Jews, though no doubt with oratorical exaggeration, as "dogs" and "swine"'.) But if we agree that the words of Christ are of significance for more than a handful of first-century Galileean bumpkins, we must imagine that they have an applicability beyond their local confines of time and place.

Certainly the human race, in its muddled and various way, has found that they do. His words are read aloud all over the world; and day by day, they win and trouble more human hearts. They teach us not to be attached to the world, certainly. But they come to us before we have even begun the quest for perfection which Tolstoy made his life. They come as a challenge. And what we can be grateful for in the prophecy of Tolstoy is that he sharpened the edge of their challenge, and made it if possible, even more unreasonable than Jesus did himself. But because of Tolstoy's obsessive simplicity, and his desire to distance himself as far as possible from the teachings of the Russian Orthodox Church, he omits whole passages of the Gospels from consideration. 'The Sermon on the Mount or the Creeds. It is impossible to believe them both'. . . . 'The teaching of the Church with its redemption and its sacraments, excludes Christ's teaching'. . . . This is splendid rhetoric. But it lacks conviction, since he is unable to justify the criteria by which he judges certain passages in the New Testament as 'authentic' and others as interpolations by the priests and theologians. Tolstoy was, as he said himself of Ruskin, 'one of those rare men who *think* with their hearts'. It is that which makes his prose so compelling, but it does not answer all the tangled implications which follow from his renunciation of the world.

But the very words that inspired Tolstoy to make his renunciation of the world are greater than Tolstoy himself. There was more in the words of Jesus than a simple moral code. We fail to keep his commandments because they go against all that our natural instincts crave – revenge, security, wealth and gratification. Tolstoy was never grander than when he said 'Blame me and not the path I tread', to those who mocked at his failures. But he failed to recognise the great body of stories and sayings in the Gospels which speak of these failures.

Jesus was not a *guru* who taught a counsel of perfection and then remained on the mountainside communing with his Heavenly father. As Saint Matthew has arranged the story, he comes down the slope and is immediately caught up with the crowds, clamouring for healing. He heals a leper. Then he heals the centurion's servant. Then he heals the mother-in-law of Peter. Then, once more, the awesome demands. 'Foxes have holes and the birds of the air their resting-places; the Son of Man has nowhere to lay his head'. He tells a man that he should not even delay by going to his father's funeral. 'Leave the dead to bury their dead' (Matthew 8:20, 23). As if to emphasise the extraordinary gap between human weakness and the demands of perfection which Jesus places upon his disciples, Matthew then devotes the opening of his ninth chapter to two stories.

In the first, a palsied bed-ridden man is carried to Jesus, who tells him that his sins are forgiven. When the scribes protest against this, he says, 'To convince you that the Son of Man has authority to forgive sins while he is on earth. . . . Rise up, take thy bed with thee, and go home'. (Matthew 9:6). We may assume that all three writers of the synoptic gospels attached great importance to this story, for they all tell it, and in roughly the same form. Its import is obvious. Of course it is a theological understanding, or interpretation of the importance of Jesus which has made them tell the story, and to tell it in that particular way. We can even say if we like that the early Church, who believed that Jesus, in his death, had saved the world from their sins, 'made this story up'. But what was it in *him* which made them want to do so? Since they bothered to record his counsels of perfection on the Mountain, we may assume that the early Christians were as puzzled and as awe-struck as we are by their all-consuming demands. It would have been possible to suppress the 'five commandments' from all the gospel accounts if that was what the evangelists wished to do. In fact, they repeat them lavishly. But they also give us another picture, another set of stories and pictures, and I cannot see by what logical standard we accept the Sermon on the Mount as the true words of Jesus, and these other elements in the Gospel as make-believe. For after the healing of the palsied man, we are told another story. And in the light of all that has gone before in Saint Matthew's narrative, it is extremely surprising.

> As he passed further on his way, Jesus saw a man called Matthew sitting at work in the customs-house, and said to him, Follow me; and Matthew rose from his place and followed him. And afterwards, when he was taking a meal in the house, many publicans and sinners were to be found at table with him and his disciples. The Pharisees saw this, and asked his disciples, How comes it that your master eats with publicans and sinners? Jesus heard it, and said, It is not those who are in health that have need of the physician, it is those who are sick.

> (Matthew 9:9–12)

A lot of modern scholars have wondered whether Jesus was an Essene, one of the celibate ascetics who lived in a monastery on the shores of the Dead Sea. The scrolls which survived from their monastery undiscovered until our own century, have much in common with many of the New Testament writings. Whether or not he came from this monastery, Jesus obviously taught the highest and most demanding forms of asceticism, which only a comparatively few people in the history of the world, such as Tolstoy, have had the moral energy to imitate or pursue. We should expect such a person to mix only with fellow-ascetics; and, since he was so scathing about the values of this world, to keep himself unspotted from it. But in this story, we see the very reverse of what we should expect. It is not that he condones the sin. We are told that he made the very remarkable claim of being able to blot it out; that he could 'heal' the sins of Matthew and his low friends, just as he could heal the limbs of the palsied man on his stretcher. The Pharisees, we may assume, are much closer in their high ideals of purity and perfection to Jesus than the publicans and the sinners are. But it is at the table of the sinners that the gospel depicts him. Having said *Blessed are the clean of heart* and enunciated a way of perfection which, in all the generations preceding Tolstoy, has inspired men and women to renounce the world, to live in caves and on the tops of pillars, to sell all their goods and give to the poor, to starve and fast, and pray without ceasing, Jesus is seen, not in a monastic cave on the shores of the dead sea but in the boozy atmosphere of a vulgar dinner party. It is a comfort to find him there, but it is also a shock, more stunning to me, even than the initial impact of re-reading his Sermon with fresh eyes.

CHAPTER THREE

Forgiveness

In the middle of the Sermon on the Mount, with all its high counsels of perfection, Saint Matthew places The Lord's Prayer. Saint Luke (eleventh chapter) places the prayer in a rather different setting, in which the disciples actually ask, 'Lord teach us how to pray'. (Luke 11:1). Matthew's setting of the prayer emphasises what a central part forgiveness plays in the teaching of Jesus. We are not told merely, as Tolstoy, in his more fervent moods appeared to think, that we must forgive our enemies, to turn the other cheek and to refrain from resisting evil. We *are* told this. But we are also told to pray, *Forgive us our trespasses as we forgive them that trespass against us.*

Matthew obviously believed that in order to obtain the forgiveness of God, we must ourselves exercise forgiveness. In the eighteenth chapter of the Gospel, we have Peter's question, 'Lord, how often must I see my brother do me wrong, and still forgive him; as much as seven times?' with its hyperbolic answer, 'I tell thee to forgive, not seven wrongs but seventy times seven'. And there then follows the story of the unmerciful servant, who, having been forgiven all his debt to his master (some ten thousand talents) goes out and exacts a hundred pieces of silver from a fellow servant.

And so he was summoned by his master, who said to him, I remitted all that debt of thine, thou wicked servant, at thy entreaty; was it not thy duty to have mercy on thy fellow-servant, as I had mercy on thee? And his master, in anger, gave him over to be tortured until the debt was paid. It is thus that my heavenly father will deal with you, if brother does not forgive brother with all his heart.

(Matthew 18:32–35)

This is stern. But beside this saying, and the very similar one in the Sermon on the Mount (Matthew 6:14), we read of Jesus pronouncing forgiveness upon the sick, and healing of soul to the publicans and sinners in the house of Matthew the tax-gatherer. We can turn to God and pray for forgiveness. Placed in the middle of the Sermon on the Mount, the Lord's Prayer seems to say that the way of perfection cannot be accomplished without God's help. But it retains a moral, spiritual paradox. In so far as we fail to keep these commandments, we move away from God. But it is when we so move that we most need his forgiveness. You cannot serve God and money. But it is to the man who serves Money – Matthew – that Jesus himself comes.

It is our inability to keep the counsels of perfection in the Sermon which alerts us to the great distance between ourselves and God. Jesus says, 'But you are to be perfect, as your heavenly Father is perfect'. (Matthew 5:48). He knows that divine perfection is impossible for human beings, for the heart of man, left to itself, is full of anger and lust. (Matthew 5:20–32). This perfection can only be obtained by calling out to God as if he were Our Father – Abba, the familiar word used by children when addressing their earthly parents.

If any one of yourselves is asked by his son for bread, will he give him a stone? If he is asked for a fish, will he give him a serpent instead? Why then, if you, evil as you are, know well enough how to give your children what is good for them, is not your father in heaven much more ready to give wholesome gifts to those who ask him?

(Matthew 7:9–11)

So, the prayer to Our Father for forgiveness, and our pursuit of the counsels of perfection go hand in hand. We cannot be forgiven if we wilfully refuse to follow those counsels. If we are ourselves incapable of forgiving, we will soon lose any sense that we need to be forgiven. The Sermon – and Saint Matthew's Gospel as a whole – has a number of very forthright references to hell, torture, punishment and so on. But as well as Jesus's story of the angry judge and the unmerciful servant, we also have his injunction to call God, Father. It is our refusal to follow the counsels of Heaven – set out in the Sermon – which will make it impossible for us to follow God; not God's desire to reject us. This is emphasised in the sad story of the rich young man who comes up to Jesus and asks 'Master, who art so good, what good must I do to win eternal life?' The reply is surprising for those who like to believe that Jesus walked about the Galilean countryside proclaiming himself the Second Person of a Trinity in which none of his fellow-Jews believed. 'Why dost thou come to me to ask of goodness? God is good and he only'. But Jesus then advises the young man, who has kept all the outward forms of the Jewish law from his youth up, 'If thou hast a mind to be perfect, go home and sell all that belongs to thee; give it to the poor, and so the treasure thou hast shall be in heaven; then come back and follow me'. There could be no starker, no more direct application than the teachings on poverty from the Sermon. 'When he heard this, the young man went away sad at heart, for he had great possessions'. (Matthew 19:22).

From all that has gone before in this gospel, we feel the full heaviness and wretchedness of that parting. Jesus makes clear that eternal life depends on a complete stripping of oneself before God, an abandonment of earthly possessions. The young man goes away. Who should blame him? But he goes away, in so doing, from God. He has rejected God. Self-sufficient in his own virtue, as in his own riches, he can not, as the publicans and sinners can, pray for forgiveness. He can only turn away. The story is a very disturbing one for any of us who has *not* made the great renunciation. It is mere casuistry to say that Jesus only told *this particular young man* to sell all his goods. We might as well say that Jesus in general approved of leprosy but only cured this or that particular leper. The young man is judged by his refusal to keep the counsels of perfection enunciated by Jesus. And he executes the judgement himself. He walks away.

But, even in St Matthew, the sternest of all the New Testament writers, there is the strong implication that the meaning of *repentance* is to be found in our *attempt*, however feeble, to keep the commandments. It is those who are sick, not those who are well, who need the doctor. The young man does not fall at the feet of Jesus and say, 'I can not rid my heart of its love of earthly possession. Help me to do so'. He just walks away. By implication, he denies, not his ability to follow Christ, but Christ himself. That is his condemnation. That is what Jesus, as depicted by the evangelists, finds repellent in the Pharisees. The contrast is well-illustrated by the story in St Luke's Gospel.

There were some who had confidence in themselves, thinking they had won acceptance with God, and despised the rest of the world; to them he addressed this other parable: Two men went up into the temple to pray; one was a Pharisee, the other a publican. The Pharisee stood upright and made this prayer in his heart, I thank thee, God, that I am not like the rest of men, who steal and cheat and commit adultery, or like this publican here; for myself, I fast twice in the week, I give tithes of all that I possess. And the publican stood far off; he would not even lift up his eyes towards heaven; he only beat his breast, and said, God be merciful to me; I am a sinner. I tell you, this man went back home higher in God's favour than the other. . . .

(Luke 18:9–14)

The sinners and publicans with whom Jesus is said to have consorted were not, of course, closer to God in their behaviour. The Pharisee, like the rich young man, has kept all the law. From Matthew's gospel, at least, we would infer that

36

a failure to keep the law of God will distance us from God. If the Pharisee's deviation was minimal, or non-existent and the Publican's was great, why was the Publican justified? It is certainly not because Jesus taught moral libertinism. He said that if the justice of his disciples did not exceed the justice of the scribes and pharisees they would not enter the kingdom (Matthew 5:20). The only way in which the publican was preferred to the pharisee is that he recognised his dependence on God. This is a fundamental principle in his manifesto for the Kingdom. The lilies of the field rely on God to clothe them. The birds of the air peck at seeds as they need them; they do not gather into barns. Without the benefit of intelligence, they depend simply upon God. How much more, in the moral life, do human beings depend upon God, to purify them and to forgive them. Paradoxically, it is very often the impure who recognise this more than the pure. For a high standard of moral behaviour, just as great riches, creates the illusion of human independence and self-sufficiency.

But why is this an illusion? What is wrong with thinking ourselves responsible for our own actions? Surely the Pharisee *was* better than the Publican, closer, even, in his standards and behaviour to Jesus's own ideals of perfection? The story of the encounter with the rich young man is outrageous, really. A perfectly decent young man approaches and asks for counsel. He makes it very clear that he is a *good* young man. There may be something very smug about him, but if he is as virtuous as he says he is, he deserves to be smug. He is asked to do something which is quite unreasonable: to give up all his worldly possessions. He rejects the advice and, by implication, is condemned.

It is when we contemplate the figure of this young man, or the Pharisees at other junctures in the Gospels (who are nearly always represented as types of virtue or strict upholders of the *law*) that one starts to doubt Jesus's *right* to make these claims and demands. He offers an ideal of perfection which almost anyone in their senses would reject. But he then offers us *forgiveness* if we accept the desirability of the ideal. If we try to forgive others, we will be forgiven; if we are sick and recognise our need to be healed, he will heal us. It is therefore not merely the offer of forgiveness, but the ideal of perfection which can reconcile us to God. Dare we infer that our failures, our backslidings, our stumblings into the ditch (to use Tolstoy's phrase) will be forgiven so long as we are on the right road? Forgiveness is not withdrawn from the man who himself withholds forgiveness because of Divine pique. It is withheld because he is not in a position to receive it. The man who loves Money can not love God. 'For where your treasure is, there will your heart be also'. Even if, in each man and woman, the renunciation of wealth, the vows to be chaste, to give up vengeance, and violence, take different forms, they must be made, the Jesus of St Matthew's Gospel would seem to say, before we can approach God. In other words, forgiveness makes higher demands upon us than if we were not forgiven. The rich young man turned away sorrowful, but he was able to pursue his own ideal of perfection without reference to Jesus. Those who would enter 'the Kingdom' must do so on Jesus's terms and not their own.

Am I speaking metaphorically? The words of the Lord's prayer are so familiar to me that I have hardly ever paused to ask what I mean by the phrase *forgive us our trespasses*. Obviously, I know that I have fallen short, in many ways and on many occasions, not merely in the pursuit of Jesus's ideals of perfection, but by the standards of ordinary common decency. I do not dispute that I have done wrong things in my life, said wrong things, thought and felt wrong things. I can not be like the Pharisee in the Temple nor like the rich young man and claim that I have been blameless. I have therefore quite often assumed that I was like the Publican. *Lord have mercy on me, a sinner*. Of course, the words and the story have a very high emotional appeal.

Do I believe that unless I say these words, *forgive us our trespasses*, I shall be punished by a vengeful God and sent to hell? Is it not, on the contrary, to recognise that one is more like a publican but *aspire to be* more like the Pharisee?

As I ask myself the question, I am once more in the train, and the headlines of the newspaper shout across at me.

RAPED THEN RAPED AGAIN AS SHE SOUGHT HELP says one. PORN VIDEO THAT WRECKED A FAMILY and MAN FOUND MURDERED decorate page 5; on page 9 we find RAID ON MUSEUM and on page 11 BOY HUNG BY ANKLES. The familiar collection of horror with which Londoners are greeted each evening as they come out of work. The man who brought home the 'porn video that wrecked a family' broke down and wept in court. So, probably, will the rapists and the murderers and the person or persons who hung up the boy by his ankles. But the victims of all this exuberant human behaviour would probably prefer the world to be inhabited by smug pharisees than repentant sinners. How can such outrages, in human terms, be forgiven? How is life tolerable if they are not? All these disgusting newspaper stories do nothing to contradict the Sermon on the Mount, which warns us of the dangers of violence and lust in our hearts. But how can we speak of forgiveness of these things, without trivialising our whole sense of justice, and without ignoring the vision of the divine law which Jesus offers us in the Sermon? How, in short, can Jesus forgive sin without condoning it. And what can we mean by his power to forgive *our* sin?

Geza Vermes, in his book *Jesus the Jew* points out that in some of the old Qumran texts, found among the scrolls of the Dead Sea, the phrase 'to forgive sins' was synonymous with 'to heal', and he mentions several charismatic Jewish healers who spoke as if healing and forgiveness were one and the same thing. But all the New Testament Books are written by men who believed that Jesus's power to forgive sin was something much more universal than his isolated pronouncements of healing in rural Galilee. If one is not a Jew, particularly if one is not a first century Jew with at least a folk-memory of the blood-sacrifices in the Temple at Jerusalem, it is very hard to adopt the world-picture upon which so much of the New Testament phraseology of forgiveness is dependent. The Epistle to the Hebrews, for instance, believes that the death of Jesus was not merely analogous to the old blood-offerings; it was their completion. For he was the only perfect High Priest who did not need to make a blood offering for his own sins. He was in fact both Priest and Victim. 'By a single offering he has completed his work, for all time, in those whom he sanctifies'. We are therefore 'saved' from our sins by his blood. But, if we once lapse into sin again after we have been sanctified, there is no possibility of being redeemed.

> We can do nothing for those who have received, once for all, their enlightenment, who have tasted the heavenly gift, partaken of the Holy Spirit, known, too, God's word of comfort, and the powers that belong to a future life, and then fallen away. They cannot attain repentance through a second renewal. Would they crucify the Son of God a second time, hold him up to mockery a second time, for their own ends?

> (Hebrews 6:4–6)

But St Paul, writing to the Corinthians, takes a less harsh view of Christians who have sinned. Clearly one of the Christians in the riotously badly-behaved congregation at Corinth had gone too far. In the first epistle, St Paul alludes to a man who has married his step-mother and upbraids the Corinthians for not excommunicating him. But in his second epistle, whether alluding to this man or another, he appears to have changed his mind.

> This punishment inflicted on him by so many of you is punishment enough for the man I speak of, and now you must think rather of shewing him indulgence, and comforting him; you must not let him be overwhelmed by excess of grief.

> (II Corinthians 2:6–8)

This is not a mere matter of church discipline. For St Paul, it lay at the very heart of his Gospel, which he reiterates in all his epistles, but never more movingly than in this same second letter to Corinth:

It follows, in fact, that when a man becomes a new creature in Christ, his old life has disappeared, everything has become new about him. This, as always, is God's doing; it is he who, through Christ, has reconciled us to himself, and allowed us to minister this reconciliation of his to others. Yes, God was in Christ, reconciling the world to himself, establishing in our hearts his message of reconcilation, instead of holding them to account for their sins.

(II Corinthians 5:17–19)

Since the whole of early Christianity is dominated by the overpowering vision, theology and genius of St Paul, and we feel his influence even in documents, such as St Matthew which are probably reacting *against* his libertarianism, it is almost impossible to establish whether Jesus expounded a scheme of forgiveness in anything like Pauline terms. St Paul, having been a rabid upholder of the Jewish law, came to see that, even if it were kept in all its perfection it could not reconcile us to God. From the Epistle to the Romans, in which he expounds his theme most fully, it would seem that some such reflection as Tolstoy's was what led him to this violently unTolstoyan conclusion. Tolstoy, who hated St Paul, was to write,

A man who believes in salvation through faith in the redemption or the sacraments, cannot employ all his strength in applying Christ's moral teaching in his life.

But, as Tolstoy himself saw, the way of total perfection is unattainable. Christ's call to perfection in the Sermon on the Mount, particularly his call to be pure in heart, only emphasises our distance from God. Christ calls us to be clean of heart, St Paul would say (though he does not actually quote the beatitude) because he wants to make us clean. God alone can purify us. We can not do so through our own actions. To accept this, is not an abrogation of moral duty. The struggle to be perfect still goes on. But to accept that, forgiveness, the

41

forgiveness of God, is wholly necessary. For it is in our very struggle for perfection that we discover our inadequacy. It was because Paul was such a *good* Jew, and not because he was a bad one, that he came to believe that the Law could do more than condemn him to death. 'Pitiable creature that I am, who is to set me free from a nature thus doomed to death? Nothing else than the grace of God, through Jesus Christ Our Lord' (Romans 7:24). From this text, and indeed from the whole epistle emanates the core of what most of us recognise as Christianity. By rights, the whole world should be condemned by the old Jewish Celestial Judge. But the price of that condemnation was paid by his son, Jesus Christ. From this Epistle, the Christian Church renews itself and upsets itself from generation to generation. It was the crucial text for Luther, for Calvin, for Wesley. Indeed, almost the only major 'heretic' or reformer who felt called to rescue Christianity from the Church and was not inspired by the writings of St Paul was Tolstoy. And it is this, quite apart from any other considerations, which make his religious ideas so violently different and exciting.

Tolstoy had a much clearer picture of Jesus and his teaching than many modern New Testament scholars would think legitimate. But if, as I have said, it is the *words of Jesus* which so compel our attention, and draw us back with such repeated awe and puzzlement to the New Testament, Saint Paul comes as something of a shock. Historically, however, it is to him that we owe our very knowledge of Christ. It is impossible, therefore, not to view the apostle with reverence and gratitude, in spite of all his obvious faults of character, and in spite of his occasional foolish or incomprehensible sayings.

Paul, in the earliest extant Christian writings, speaks of forgiveness rather than dwelling upon Christ's moral teachings. In his world-view, the whole human race was condemned to death as a result of Adam's transgression (Romans 5:12 etc). The law of Moses (by implication *any* moral code) does not redeem us from our faults. All this, perhaps, seems fairly far removed from anything that could be proved, still less from what might be thought of as common human experience. But even Saint Paul seems to have a recollection of some of the sayings of Jesus, when he says, for instance that 'the man who loves his neighbour has done all that the law demands' (Romans 13:8). Although it is chiefly of the old Jewish Torah that he writes, he seems to suggest that he has some acquaintanceship, doubtless through the oral traditions of the Christians whom he eventually met, of the high ethical demands that Jesus made on his disciples. If to the old Torah, how much more to the new law of Love is St Paul's exclamation applicable: 'praiseworthy intentions are always ready to hand, but I cannot find my way to the performance of them; it is not the good my will prefers, but the evil my will disapproves, that I find myself doing'. (Romans 7:18).

We are back, for an instant, with Tolstoy, struggling to fulfil the commandment of Jesus and failing. When Tolstoy failed, he felt that he should blame himself, and not the path that he had chosen; but that he should pick himself up and struggle on once more. St Paul, with a pronounced sense of the irredeemable quality of human nature, thought that 'picking oneself up' was no way out of the difficulty. It did not, after all, cancel out our guilt. He introduces into the discussion a concept of legalistic absolution which to the western non-semitic mind is hard to accept. Can guilt be wiped clean by wholesale, ritual or legal gestures? Moreover, if we say that all our sins have been wiped clean by Jesus, is not Tolstoy right, and does not it diminish the urgency with which we try to apply Christ's moral teaching in our lives. 'What shall we say then? Shall we continue in sin that grace may abound' (Romans 6:1). Saint Paul raises the question himself, honestly enough, but he can not answer it. There was really no need to have raised it in the first place since it all depends on accepting the rather peculiar vision of God's justice which he had picked up, presumably, while studying the old rabbinic texts in his days as a fervent pharisee and disciple of Gamaliel.

Saint Paul having introduced this demoralising idea of sinning the more that grace may the more abound, the Synoptic writers, in their various ways, are all concerned to remind us that Jesus did teach a moral code, a way of life, a pattern of behaviour after which we should all aspire. Matthew's gospel

43

arranges these various moral sayings into 'the Sermon on the Mount'; St Luke, either independently, or basing himself on Matthew, does the same. But in all three Gospels, Matthew, Mark and Luke, the sayings and words of Jesus remain, though the evangelists differ in the extent to which they promise punishment (hell, rejection from the Kingdom, etc.) to those who do not keep Christ's commandments.

We can be justified in the feelings of impatience which inevitably well to the surface when contemplating the New Testament teaching on forgiveness. In various ways, they make it the very centre of the 'Good News' which they all preach. But none of them define what it is, or say what Jesus, precisely, taught about it. Perhaps he did not teach precisely about it. None of them – not Jesus, not the evangelists, not St Paul, were moral philosophers. And the attempt to pry into the meaning of these unanalytical texts is bound to lead to frustration. For having acknowledged that neither Hebrews, nor St Paul, nor the Synoptic Gospels quite give us a finished theology of forgiveness, it is not true to say that they give us no *picture*. The picture is, in fact, extraordinarily coherent, given the jumble through which we approach it. And if we approach it as if for the first time, as if a stranger who knew nothing of the Christian tradition, the picture is a totally extraordinary one. For they all – Paul, Hebrews, the Synoptics and, the glory of New Testament writings, the Johannine texts – say the same.

Return for the moment to Tolstoy, for he reads the New Testament with such fresh eyes. He is like an eager and highly intelligent child, devoid of preconceptions, seizing it and reading it from the beginning of Saint Matthew's Gospel to the end. And the first thing which arrests him, and fills him with awe, is the gravity of Christ's moral demands upon the human race. He is not the first to be arrested in this way. In every generation, there have been people who have seen the simple force of what Thomas à Kempis saw: 'If you would understand Christ's words fully and taste them truly, you must strive to form your whole life after His pattern'.

It is the simplicity of this which makes it right; also, which

44

makes its appeal, oddly enough, to the intellect. For, sooner or later in some other part of the New Testament, one is going to come across a miraculous tale which at that moment the mind refuses to swallow, or a particularly muddled or crazy passage in St Paul which the intelligence feels bound to reject. The Sermon on the Mount can not be rejected as mere foolish idealism with such ease. And its absolutism, repellent to some, is precisely what would make it attractive to others, to people of Tolstoy's temper, for instance.

Jesus, in Saint Matthew's Gospel, is not, as I have said, an ascetic guru who merely teaches his disciples an impossibly high code to follow. He tells them that they can not see God until they are pure. He tells them that they can not be forgiven until they forgive. But the evangelist always places the figure of Jesus next to the feeblest figures in humanity: the sick, the social outcasts and the morally destitute. St Matthew's Jesus does not simply say, 'I have told you the way of everlasting life; follow it, or you will go to hell.' He says, 'It is not those who are in health that have need of the physician, it is those who are sick'. (Matthew 9:12). He says, 'Come to me all you that labour and are burdened; I will give you rest'. (Matthew 11:28). Moral failure and sickness are resolved, not by some complicated scheme of Law and Cosmology as might have occurred to the over-heated intellect of the Apostle Paul. They are not resolved in a moral, or amoral scheme of 'wiping the slate clean' by some system of priestly or ritual absolution. The sick and the sinners, with their sickness and imperfection, are asked to come to Jesus.

Saint Mark arranges the material even more clearly in his opening chapter. For there we have no stories of Jesus's childhood, no reference to his origins or birth, but simply Saint John the Baptist, preaching in the desert the arrival of the Kingdom. Then Jesus comes to receive Baptism by John; he calls the disciples (*Follow me* (Mark 1:17)) and he goes into the synagogue at Capernaum where he 'amazes' the congregation with his teaching. (Mark 1:22). Unlike St Matthew, St Mark does not tell us what this teaching was until later in his Gospel, for he moves straight away into the healing stories. At evening, when the sun was set, the whole city comes crowding to his door. He departs into desert places to hide. But Peter tells him *All men are looking for thee*. (Mark 1:38)

The theme could be discovered in every chapter of Saint Mark, that repentance and a rediscovery of God are to be learnt in coming to Jesus. No amount of scholarship could ever establish how many of these sayings were 'authentic'. That is to say, no one can know how often, or in what circumstances, Jesus actually said to people that he was the means by which sickness was healed and sin was forgiven. The stories of his saying so are repeated so often that I would be surprised if none of them were based on the real memories of those who heard him preach, and heal, and astonish the crowds in the infinitely obscure villages of that tiny province of the Roman Empire. It would not disturb me to think that Jesus did not understand what he was talking about himself: the significance of his call to the sick and the sinful to come to *him* for forgiveness could certainly not have been appreciated by any who heard him at the time. But as the stories come to us, the call to repentance (and the exposition of the new Christian code of morality) are all inextricably linked to the attraction of Jesus himself. So that now, even though it does not profit us to reconstruct pictures of what he looked like, or how he sounded, we can not ignore the fact that – as they survive to us – the sayings of Jesus call us not merely to follow his words, but to come to him as to the physician of our souls.

Even in the Gospel with the most 'advanced' Christology – that of Saint John – the paradox of this is not lost or hidden. John makes no secret, from the very opening word of his Gospel, that he identifies this obscure Galilean figure with the eternal creative person of God, the everlasting Word, who was with God from the beginning of time and who was, as it were, the side of God's nature that had made the world. But it is as if to emphasise almost the humour of his claim, that John introduces us at once to the contemptuous question of Nathaniel: 'Can anything that is good come from Nazareth?' (John 1:46). Moreover, in spite of the universal claims made for the person and nature of Jesus Christ in this Gospel, it does not forebear to mention a story which, because it is so puzzlingly out of keeping with the theology of the book (at first glance) compels us to think that it is, *faute de mieux*, a memory of a genuine saying of Jesus.

It is the story in the fourth chapter of Saint John in which Jesus finds himself wandering through the alien territory of the Samaritans, near Jacob's Well at Sichar. It is hard to believe that the conversation which follows has been recorded in a Boswellian fashion – who could have recorded it? Not the woman, and not Jesus, who, blessed be his Holy Name, wrote no books. It is a reconstructed dialogue, of a platonic pattern, as are all the great chapters of St John. But it contains *nuggets*. As with all things in Saint John, a very ordinary thing – a man sitting on a well and asking for a drink of water – becomes something which is totally extraordinary – the promise that Jesus can give the water of life.

Anyone who drinks such water as this will be thirsty again afterwards, the man who drinks the water I give him will not know thirst any more.

(John 4:13)

But even in the midst of this highly mystical dialogue, the two fall to discussing the differences between the Samaritans and the Jews. Jesus avers that 'Salvation after all, is to come from the Jews' (John 4:22). 'You worship you cannot tell what, we worship knowing what it is we worship.' This exchange is so contrary to the mystical tenor of the whole conversation that it is hard not to think of it as an awkwardly authentic *logion* of Jesus himself.

But, the author of the Gospel has Jesus add, 'the time is coming, nay, has already come, when true worshippers will worship the Father in spirit and in truth'. In miniature, we can see in this story, perhaps, three processes by which the great Johannine vision of Christ emerges. On the one hand, perhaps, a genuine memory that Jesus once deigned to talk to a Samaritan woman, sitting by Jacob's well. He told her,

47

perhaps, that salvation is of the Jews. He told her, perhaps, that she was wrong to have five husbands. It is even possible that some talk about the water of life passed between them. But what we see is simply Jesus of Nazareth sitting with a woman. Those who witnessed it 'were surprised to find him talking to a woman' (John 4:27). But that is all they would have seen.

Even embedded into the story, though, however much the Johannine writer has elaborated or made up, is the invitation to come to Jesus. He discloses the woman's own sins to her. She goes into the town and says, 'Come and have a sight of the man who has told me all the story of my life'.

We have, growing out of this dual side to the story – the events and words themselves, the call to *come to him* – the Johannine writer's sense of the incident's significance. In this Gospel, Jesus actually announces himself to the woman, as the Christ (John 4:26).

In all the Gospels, then, differently as they present the material, there is the presence of a group of sayings or stories which emphasise the same belief: that Jesus did not simply enunciate a moral code which was to be followed; he offers himself to be our helper when we fail to live up to that standard. He tells the disciples in Saint Matthew to be pure in heart; but in his turning to the sinners and calling them to him, as a physician would call the sick, he makes it clear that purity of heart is not a pre-requisite of the Christian life; it is its consequence. We become pure, as he purifies us. And *then* we see God. In Saint John, the same point is made by the story of the Samaritan woman at the well. It is Jesus who gives the water of life. It is Jesus who sees the woman's imperfections, both because she is a Samaritan outside the organised pale of Jewish religion, and because she is an adulteress. There is then the declaration that he is the Christ, the one who is to reveal the true worship of God to the human race.

The purposes of the Gospels were, of course, to instruct the faithful, to provide illustrations of preconceived religious ideas about Jesus. They are not objective, still less biographical, accounts, and to extract from them any 'objective' saying or truth about some putative 'historical Jesus' has been a task which has always ended in failure. We only have the Jesus in whom the evangelists believed, and in whom Paul believed. The significance of the real historical Jesus saying, 'Come to me' or 'follow me' or 'I came to heal the sick' can not possibly have been understood or interpreted theologically at the time. His ministry, whatever it was exactly, was exercised almost entirely in the countryside and in remote villages. The healings, the exorcism and the preaching have been compared with that of other Jewish 'charismatics'. The pardon, healing and strengthening of God came to the sick or (which was in those days synonymous) to the sinful through the hands of the holy man. This particular Galilean holy man drew up a Way of Holiness of searching austerity. But, intertwined with this Way, are the collection of sayings which seem to say that it may not be followed without him. In Saint John's Gospel this intertwining reaches its consummation with the announcement: 'I am the way, I am truth and life' (John 14:6).

The other rabbis, charismatics, prophets, monks and teachers passed out of memory, or into the history of the Jewish writers alone. The story of the Galilean who preached the Sermon on the Mount becomes the story of a universal healer. He is not one who forgives sins in the way that sin was forgiven with the old temple-rites of blood-sprinkling. He reveals the heart of man as something which, in every individual case, is in need of purification and healing. And he proposes himself as the healer. That, anyhow, is how the followers of the Way chose to present him when they came to write down their necessarily finite, necessarily imperfect accounts of the Good News. A very big claim for an itinerant exorcist in the northern province of Palestine. Perhaps we do not believe that it was a claim which he made for himself. In that case, it is more and not less remarkable that the claim should have been made for him, and in such grandiose terms after he had suffered the criminal execution normally meted out to slaves.

Why did they make such claims? It is sometimes said that religious belief is the result of 'wish-fulfilment'. We believe in one who conquered death because we can not tolerate the

horror of permanent extinction. We are so neurotically tor-
mented with guilt that we need the healing mumbo-jumbo of
a religion to cleanse and restore us. That may be so. In fact, we
can be fairly certain that it is so; and that the human race, being
so largely made up of unhappy and imperfect individuals, has
fashioned Christ in its own image again and again. Christ can
become an idol, just as any other God, or non-God can be,
when seen through the blinkered and distorted vision of
human understanding.

But what 'wishes' did Jesus 'fulfil'? He came to Jerusalem,
perhaps with the false reputation of a troublemaker, but as a
wholly obscure freelance Galileean rabbi, exorcist or preacher.
He came to a religious capital, and to a Temple, which had as
highly elaborate a system of cleansing from unrighteousness,
as any religion in the world. If you were a Jew who believed in
God and wanted him to forgive you your sins, would you not
follow the procedures laid down, rather than following a man
who had not merely suffered criminal execution, but also in
his lifetime acquired the character of one who despised the
notion of formal ritual cleansing? He had been said on more
than one occasion (Nain and Lazarus) to touch a corpse. He
disputed the necessity to indulge in ritual washings before
meals, and had even given utterance to the extraordinarily
crude observation that we are made filthy not by the food
which comes into our mouths but by the waste products
which come out of us at the other end.

Forget the religious crackpots nowadays. If one were a first
century *Jew*, consumed with the wish to be cleansed and
purified of all unrighteousness, would one come to this dead
man for such purification, rather than going to the Temple,
and showing oneself to the priests? It is said that Jesus's chief
appeal among the Jews was to those such as the taxgatherers
and other 'sinners' who were outlaws from Jewry and could
therefore not get the cleansing and absolution which the
temple ceremonies offered. But we find among his followers
high-ranking Jews such as Nicodemus and Joseph of Ari-
mithea; we find, even after his death, that his disciples are
temple-going Jews; we find the most enthusiastic convert to

the new Way is that Hebrew of Hebrews, Saul of Tarsus. It is these men, these Jews, who for some reason eventually became convinced that Jesus was the saviour not merely of Jewry but of the human race; that Jesus had taught a new and perfect way of life; a new way of praying; a new way of reconciling the irreconcilable: imperfect man and perfect God. As a fantasy buzzing alone in the mind of Saint Paul, it would be odd enough. As a lunatic but pathetic delusion on the part of his small band of Galilean admirers and friends, it would be understandable. Saint Paul makes a point of saying that these two violently opposed groups (himself and the Galileans) reached their conclusions quite independently. If we can believe in the Acts of the Apostles, it would seem that the first followers of Jesus, gathered in Jerusalem, did indeed begin to practise a 'Tolstoyan' form of Christianity, giving up their money, holding all things in common, and living at peace with the world.

We find Peter, who had denied Jesus at the time of his trial, reported as preaching:

Repent, Peter said to them, and be baptized, every one of you, in the name of Jesus Christ, to have your sins forgiven;

(Acts 2:38)

Jesus himself is the means of forgiveness. Leading a good life; leading, indeed, a life of moral perfection. That is one aspect of the Way. Learning to approach the creator of earth, moon and sky and to address Him with the familiarity of a child addressing its father; that is another aspect; regretting our imperfection and finding a healer for our fallen nature. All three are gathered up in him who said he *was* the Way.

The Christian experience of forgiveness, the Christian's aspiration to be good, the Christian's attempt to pray, they are all, in the repeated experiences of Christians down the centuries, something which turns out to have been an encounter with a person. Perhaps they begin with the excitement of an idea – the idea of living a life of Tolstoyan simplicity, perhaps, or the *idea* of reconciling the jarring factions of the human race through the power of love. It ends, always, in the experience of a person. There are so many accounts of it that there is no particular need to quote any one of them. As far as one can tell, these personal encounters have gone on for the last nineteen hundred years: baffling to those who take a benevolent attitude towards them, straightly unbelievable to the majority who have ever heard of them. I am not talking merely of wild visions, the lunatic flights of 'mystical experience' which is not mystical at all. I am thinking of the simple conviction which occurs to non-lunatics, and non-visionaries, that they have been in the presence of the Lord. No one perhaps has made the encounter more vivid than the seventeenth century poet George Herbert.

> Love bade me welcome: yet my soul drew back,
> Guiltie of dust and sinne.
> But quick-ey'd Love, observing me grow slack
> From my first entrance in,
> Drew nearer to me, sweetly questioning
> If I lack'd any thing.
>
> A guest I answer'd, worthy to be here:
> Love said, You shall be he.
> I the unkinde, ungratefull? Ah, my deare,
> I cannot look on thee.
> Love took my hand, and smiling did reply,
> Who made the eyes but I?
>
> Truth, Lord, but I have marr'd them: let my shame
> Go where it doth deserve.
> And know you not, sayes Love, who bore the blame?
> My deare, then I will serve.
> You must sit down, sayes Love, and taste my meat:
> So I did sit and eat.

It was during the recitation of this poem to herself in 1938 that Simone Weil became aware that the experience described by Herbert was not merely a 'poetic' but a true one.

It was during one of these recitations that, as I told you, Christ himself came down and took possession of me.

In my arguments about the insolubility of the problem of God I had never foreseen the possibility of that, of a real contact, person to person, here below, between a human being and God. I had vaguely heard tell of things of this kind, but I had never believed in them. In the *Fioretti* the accounts of the apparitions rather put me off if anything, like the miracles in the Gospel. Moreover, in this sudden possession of me by Christ, neither my senses nor my imagination had any part. . . . God in his mercy had prevented me from reading the mystics, so that it should be evident to me that I had not invented this absolutely unexpected contact.

The claims of Jesus are so absolute and so odd that we would be unsurprised that his words and sayings attracted people, who saw through the illusory nature of worldly comforts. The experience of personal encounter between perfectly intelligent, and often unimaginative people and Jesus Christ remains one of those things which baffle the world, and which will never be explained because it is not meant to be explained. It begins as a word on a page, or, more likely, a word echoing in our ear – for the words of Jesus must be the most oft-repeated of any uttered. The words are telling us to be perfect, to be pure. They seem inadmissible. *Who* he was who uttered them, no historian can ever tell us. The more they scavenge among the dismembered parts of the New Testament texts, the less the scholars seem to know, or, surprisingly, to want to know. Generations of overconfident pronouncements of what Jesus was like, how he behaved, how he was tried, and why he was put to death have muzzled the experts with embarrassment. The personal encounters of generations of people with the 'living Lord' can not be taken into account by the scholars. And rightly so, for the scholars deal only in what can be analytically verified. The believer's experience is thus both all-in-all and of no importance. It has, that is to say, no general importance at all. It proves nothing, though it indicates something about the promises, the nature, perhaps, of Jesus. Jesus is not someone we take up an interest in, as we might become interested in Kant or Aristotle or Shakespeare. For almost all those who are *most* interested in Jesus claim, with differing explanations, or total absence of explanation of what they mean, that he is still alive. He left no record whatsoever of what he was like. He wrote no book. His sayings come to us in an arrangement which was not of his own choosing. But there is one thing which tradition tells us he did, as it were, for posterity. It was perhaps the simplest and at the same time the most mysterious thing that he ever did.

CHAPTER FOUR

Bread of Heaven

Thomas Carlyle, of all the great Victorian writers, is today the least read and the least admired. But his fevered rhetorical works contain, amidst much claptrap and windbaggery, sentences of great wisdom. I like his Journal entry for June 23, 1870 when he has been reading various contemporary atheist writings.

> Cease, cease, my poor empty-minded, loud-headed, much-bewildered friends. 'Religion', this, too, God be thanked, I perceive to be again possible, to be again *here*, for whoever will piously struggle upwards, and sacredly, sorrowfully *refuse to speak lies*, which indeed will mostly mean refuse to speak at all on that topic. No words for it in our base time. In no time or epoch can the Highest be spoken of in words – not in many words, I think, *ever*. But it can even now be silently beheld, and even *adored* by whoever has eyes and adoration, *i.e.* reverence in him. . . .

His refusal to speak lies made Carlyle unwilling to attach himself to any church or to mouth theological formularies of which he had no understanding, and in that he showed himself deeply religious. Pure religion remains untouched by the flood of atheist writing that has cluttered the bookshelves since Carlyle died. And it has surely rarely been helped or furthered by the equally large volume of Christian apologetics, theology and propaganda. In our own day, multitudes of words have been wasted by theologians, or ex-theologians, telling us that the doctrine of Christ's incarnation is false, and almost as many words by the smaller number of theologians trying to tell us that it is true.

But words are not the only way of conveying religious truth; and they are perhaps not the best way. Through all our modern verbiage, the words of Jesus, few and gnomic, speak clearly and sharply, refusing to be silenced, gripping each new generation who rediscovers them, and calling us to rebuild the kingdom again in our hearts. But even the words of Jesus are sometimes muffled by our deafness and our incomprehension and our inability to perform them, and since he never wrote them down but trusted them to the fallible memories of his friends and followers, it is perhaps as well that they are not his only legacy to the world.

Those of us who remember low mass in the days before the entire Western church became addicted to liturgical change were privileged to see an embodiment (though not one that he would have approved!) of Carlyle's view that religion 'in our base time' could be best found in silence. The priest stood at the altar. No more than a murmur could be heard by the congregation. It did not matter if there were five there to witness it, or five hundred. He took bread and quietly said the words which Jesus used at the Last Supper. He did the same with the chalice of wine. He raised the host above his head. 'It can even now be silently beheld and even *adored* by whoever has eyes and adoration'. The Host was broken, and consumed.

His was the word, He spake it.
He took the bread and brake it.
And what his word doth make it,
So I believe and take it.

Few Christians would ever have disputed with Queen Elizabeth's jingle about the Holy Sacrament. It is not something which can be explained, or which *should* be explained. He did not say, 'Write books about this', or 'quarrel about this' or 'define this' nor, 'force your own interpretation of this upon people who do not share your particular patterns of thought'. He said, simply, 'do this'. It was never more eloquently apparent than in the old pattern of celebrating the Lord's Supper in almost-silence. For there, only the actions were visible, and one could concentrate upon them in all their simplicity: a man taking bread, and blessing it, giving thanks and breaking it, and eating it; a man taking a cup, giving thanks, blessing it and drinking from it.

Christianity has survived in the world by the countless repetitions of this action. St Paul, writing to the Corinthians in perhaps AD 56 or 57 says,

> The tradition which I received from the Lord, and handed on to you, is that the Lord Jesus, on the night when he was being betrayed, took bread, and gave thanks, and broke it, and said, Take, eat; this is my body, given up for you. Do this for a commemoration of me. And so with the cup, when supper was ended, This cup, he said, is the new testament, in my blood. Do this, whenever you drink it, for a commemoration of me.
>
> (I Corinthians 11:23–25)

Since Paul refers to the 'tradition', some twenty years after the death of Jesus, it would seem unduly sceptical to doubt that this tradition stretched back to the very beginnings of Christianity. In one form or another, the tradition continues to this day. Everywhere in the Christian world last Sunday morning, these actions were repeated: a man, breaking bread, and blessing a cup. Some Christians refer to these actions as 'the holy mysteries', and such they are. For nothing that was ever written or said about them could plumb their meaning. Almost every *word* of Jesus has been, not only a light to the human race, but, because the intellects of men are dim and their hearts are dark, a problem. For one thing, the original words were spoken in Aramaic, and then translated into Greek, and so they come to us who do not read those languages as it were at third hand. Then, although their meaning might seem luminously clear to us, an almost opposite meaning could be placed upon it by someone else. Thus the words of Jesus, forever challenging us to 'repentance', or 'rethinking', make our minds churn and churn about.

But in his simple memorial to the world, we are not asked to use our minds. We are asked to 'do this'. That is all. Of course, because he gave this instruction to human beings, it has been fulfilled in the most imperfect, and even scandalous way. The great schism between the churches of the East and the church of the West left Christianity divided but (except for the esoteric distinction of the *filioque* clause in the creed) very largely united in belief and practice. The Reformation in Europe, on the other hand, erupted into violently acrimonious differences about this very simple injunction to 'do this'. Europeans had not been content silently to behold, and even adore. They had yielded to the woeful temptation to *explain*. The holy mysteries had become something which theologians believed themselves capable of defining in words. Is it any wonder that, confronted with the grosser forms of medieval superstition, the tales of bleeding Hosts, the theology which made Christ's Eucharist into a sort of magic, that the Wycliffites and the Protestant reformers should have wanted to return to the purity of the Gospel? And is it any wonder, either, that those who had silently beheld and adored should have been shocked to hear the very object of their adoration dismissed as a blasphemous fable and a dangerous deceit?

Thus began the most appalling blasphemy in the history of Christendom, for which the vilest tortures and the most reckless murders were committed. To defend the mystery, the Latin church erected yet *more* definitions, and chose to punish, at best with excommunication, at worst with death, those who disputed the wording. Meanwhile, in the centuries which stretched ahead, the protestant sectaries proliferated, each with their own definition, or lack of it, of the mystery. The followers of George Fox, dismayed by the fact that such fury could be provoked by a discussion of the Sacrament, such disobedience to the peaceable commands of Christ, abandoned the sacramental life altogether, preferring to commune in their own chamber and be still; to cultivate their own 'inner light', which they called 'the candle of the Lord'.

The Quaker silence is surely preferable to the crackling fires that burnt Ridley and Latimer, or the anguished howls of Margaret Clitheroe the young Yorkshire woman who was judicially crushed to death because of her devotion to the eucharistic mystery. But Quakerism ignores the tradition which Saint Paul received and passed on to the Corinthians, a tradition recognised by almost all Christian people to this day. 'Do this for a commemoration of me'.

> Is it not enough for me to believe the words of Christ, saying, *This is my body*? And cannot I take it thankfully, and believe it heartily, and confess it joyfully; but I must pry into the secret and examine it by the rules of *Aristotle* and *Porphyry* and find out the nature and the undiscernible philosophy of the manner of its change and torment my own brains, and distract my heart, and torment my Bretheren, and lose my charity, and hazard the loss of all the benefits intended to me, by the Holy Body; because I break those few words into more questions than the holy bread is into particles to be eaten?

Those words of Jeremy Taylor's (the great seventeenth century divine) must be among the sanest ever written about the Sacrament. They emphasise moreover a truth after which I was groping in my reflexions about Christian forgiveness. It is the ethical requirements of the Way which, initially, one finds most arresting. It appears that Jesus is laying before us a new law of love after which he expects his disciples to aspire. So, surely, he was. It was not the Quaker George Fox, nor the arch-heretic Tolstoy, but rather the 'high church' non-juring saint William Law who wrote,

> that there is not one command in all the Gospel for public worship; and perhaps it is a duty that is least insisted upon in Scripture of any other. The frequent attendance at it is never so much as mentioned in all the New Testament. Whereas

that religion or devotion which is to govern the ordinary actions of our life is to be found in every verse of Scripture. Our blessed Saviour and His Apostles are wholly taken up in doctrines that relate to common life. They call us to renounce the world, and differ in every temper and way of life . . . to profess the blessedness of mourning, to seek the blessedness of poverty of spirit; to forsake the pride and vanity of riches . . . etc.

One would not wish to deny that this *is* the general tenor of all the evangelical counsels and that no Christian life could be sustained without perpetual reference to these commands. But we observed that in the arrangement of these sayings, commands and stories, the evangelists had been careful to show that Jesus was not merely instructing the disciples to follow the Way; he was the Way. In his last discourses in Saint John's Gospel, Jesus says, 'separated from me, you have no power to do anything'. (John 15:5). 'The command, "Be ye perfect", is, like all Divine commands, at the same time a promise'. Jesus calls men to perfection, but he also describes himself as their doctor. It is he who will perfect them. It seemed, from the discussions in the last chapter, as though there were not, as is popularly supposed, any necessarily clear-cut 'states' of spiritual progress. The Gospel-religion was not a mere course of self-improvement. On the other hand, without the sincere attempt to purify himself, the disciple could not hope to see God; and without a preparedness to forgive others he could not himself be forgiven. The Christian therefore, was someone who, as soon as he had responded to any part of the Gospel, would at once be caught up in all its mystery. He would not first aim at forgiving others, *then* be forgiven. He would not, either, believe himself to be forgiven and therefore decide to forgive others. He would find that both in forgiving and in being forgiven he was involved in the same mystery. At all stages, as the arrangement of the Sermon in Matthew makes clear, it is a way of prayer. We say 'Our Father' because we aspire to the Way. We only tread the Way because we can say 'Our Father'. It is Jesus who is the teacher of the Way, but also Jesus who guides and leads his followers along the Way, not those who are already quite satisfied with a completely self-sufficient religious system – the Pharisees – but those who are stumblingly aware of their own inadequacy – the Publicans and the sinners. Jesus is therefore, as the writer of the Letter to the Hebrews described him, the 'author and finisher' of faith (Hebrews 12:2 AV), or as the apocalyptic visionary at the end of the New Testament says, 'Alpha and Omega, the beginning of all things and their end'. (Apocalypse 1:8). Jesus calls, but without his co-operation, it will never be possible to make a total response.

The experience of certainty that one has met Jesus in prayer, the experience of being possessed by him, such as was described by Simone Weil on page 53 is not something which is vouchsafed to all. In fact, even believers might treat such experiences, sincerely as they are felt and described by those who have them, with the caution which must always be afforded to claims of 'religious experience'. When the wise Bishop of Durham Joseph Butler said to John Wesley, 'Sir, the pretending to gifts of the Holy Ghost is a horrid thing, a very horrid thing', he said so with the conviction that the Holy Ghost *was* the Holy Ghost, and that the divine majesty should not be trivialised by being wrapped up in a department of mere 'psychic' phenomena. It is not to *deny* that men and women have been filled with the Holy Ghost, seen visions, and known with certainty the presence of Jesus. It is to recognise that, if these experiences are authentic they are indeed gifts of God and not mere emanations of fancy. It would be surprising, if Christianity were true, had *no one* received such experiences. But it would not invalidate the traditional claims of Christianity if all such experiences could be irrefutably proved to be false. For the institution of the Eucharist, the simplicity of the action and of the command – 'do this' – does not depend upon any mystical experience at all, even though it is precisely in their experience of the Eucharist that many of the most exalted visions of the mystics have been said to come.

The Eucharist, after all, is the most eloquent enactment of all the evangelical teachings about his call to perfection, his forgiveness to those who are as yet too feeble to do more than stumble along the Way. For it is a wholly passive thing. Christians are merely asked to 'do this', to submit to this simplest of instructions, to be fed. It is the ultimate act of faith, but it is achieved not by the pursuit of a high mystical road, but simply by kneeling and having something placed in our mouths. The Jesus of St John's Gospel speaks of it with blank simplicity, and with full cognizance that its simplicity defies belief.

> It is I who am the bread of life; he who comes to me will never be hungry, he who has faith in me will never know thirst. (But you, as I have told you, though you have seen me, do not believe in me).
>
> (John 6:35–36)

Nobody, as I have said, could possibly know quite what it is that they do when they kneel and receive Holy Communion. Everything is contained in that act of receptivity. But nobody who has read the New Testament can doubt that it was Christ's command to his disciples. In one of Jeremy Taylor's most beautiful passages he expands upon this.

> All Christian people must come. They indeed that are in the state of sin must not come so, but yet they must come. First they must quit their state of death, and then partake of the bread of life. They that are at enmity with their neighbours must come, that is no excuse for their not coming; only they must not bring their enmity along with them, but leave it, and then come. They that have variety of secular employments must come, only they must leave their secular thoughts and affections behind them, and then come and converse with God. If any man be well grown in grace he must needs come, because he is excellently disposed to so holy a feast: but he that is but in the infancy of piety had need to come, so that he may grow in grace. The strong must come, lest they become weak; and the weak, that they may

62

become strong. The sick must come to be cured, the healthful to be preserved. They that have leisure must come, because they have no excuse: they that have no leisure must come hither, that by so excellent religion they may sanctify their business. The penitent sinners must come, that they may be justified, and they that are justified, that they may be justified still. They that have fears and great reverence to these mysteries, and think no preparation to be sufficient, must receive, that they may learn how to receive the more worthily; and they that have a less degree of reverence, must come often to have it heightened: that as those creatures that live amongst the snows of the mountains turn white with their food and conversation with such perpetual white-nesses, so our souls may be transformed into the similitude and union with Christ by our perpetual feeding on him, and conversation, not only in his courts, but in his very heart, and most secret affections and incomparable purities.

*

Holy Communion was, is, the tangible, visible, empirical gift of Jesus to the world. There is such simplicity and practicality in this. Even after the Christians themselves had committed the ultimate blasphemy of dividing the Body of Christ because they could not agree about definitions of the Body of Christ, the Sacrament continues. It is the great Christian sign. Doubt-less, the quality of Christian life should also be a Sign to the world, but one has only to write the words to discover how optimistic, or how hollow, they sound. Unfortunately, for every Christian life burning and illumined with Christ's love, there is another burning with something altogether different. Christians, who are called to live by a higher ideal than most other religious groups, not infrequently scandalize the rest of the world by their belligerence, their lack of charity, their air of superiority and pride, their apparent indifference, the more fervent they become, to the dictates of Jesus Christ. And a well-disposed agnostic or humanist can look askance at what the Christian revelation is supposed to teach the world. It is in living memory that, at the tomb of Christ in Jerusalem, a

Franciscan friar beat an Armenian priest to death with a broom for presuming on the strictly Latin privilege of ringing out the bells on Easter day to announce that the Lord was Risen Indeed. The news reports carry to us each day pictures of war-mongering Maronites. From Ireland, however much the peace-loving inhabitants assure us that it is not a primarily religious struggle, we see men on both sides, dressed in the garb of the clergy and apparently shedding benediction upon the murderers.

Of course, everyone recognises that this is a perversion of Christianity. Unfortunately, human sympathies, and the absence of sympathies, being what they are, it is not only the thugs and the murderers and the fanatics who fail to make an impression on the world. A good Christian minister, who appeals to his acolytes and admirers as a very fountain of grace and the embodiment of virtue will strike another observer as merely oily, smug and conceited. One sees this in the public and journalistic response to 'church leaders'. An archbishop or pope or moderator who strikes his more charitable followers as a shining light to the world will only appear to others as an ass.

St Peter, or whoever wrote the epistles which carry his name, was surely a little optimistic when he told the early church that they had become 'a chosen race, a royal priesthood, a consecrated nation'. 'Your life amidst the Gentiles must be beyond reproach; decried as malefactors, you must let them see from your honourable behaviour, what you are; they will praise God for you, when his time comes to have mercy on them'. (I Peter 2:9, 12–13). Of course, lives lit up by Christ have been potent signs in the world. Many have become Christians because of the quality of some other person's life, lit by this radiance. But many, too, have been repelled. Many unbelievers or half-believers are under the impression that they are attracted by the new testament, fascinated by the figure of Jesus, but 'put off', or worse, repelled altogether, by the Christians.

It is unfortunate. But it is true. In many circles of the Western world nowadays, however, practising Christians are not to be met with. The modern hedonist, who feels no interest in religion whatsoever, has become as dimly aware of the Christians and their activities as were the inhabitants of the Roman Empire during the first century after the death of Jesus. Occasionally some image might flicker across his television screen – a snarling Irish politician, an archbishop grinning at an airport, a pope waving from a balcony – to remind him dimly that there is a thing called Christianity and that there was a man whom men call the Christ. But for the most part, their ignorance is more total than 'engaged' or 'committed' Christians would believe possible; and I speak not merely of the uneducated, but also of the rich and the clever. This latter class, in fact, have returned to the condition of benign but patrician ignorance which characterised Pliny the Younger, one of the most attractive figures in the ancient world.

In AD 109 or 110 he was made governor of a province of north-west Turkey, Bithynia-with-Pontus, and, two or three years later, he was evidently asked to report back to the Emperor Trajan about what punishments he was finding it necessary to give to those who persisted in belonging to the illegal sect called Christian. He wrote his letter from Pontus and clearly saw nothing wrong with punishing the Christians, if necessary by death. On the whole, however, he was bound to concede that they appeared to be living innocent lives. He had not been able to find out quite what their cult was like. Apparently, they would meet on a particular day before it was light and sing some sort of hymn to Christ. They would make a sacramental vow to turn away from theft, adultery, apostasy and various other sins. There apparently followed some sort of communal eating of bread. All perfectly harmless. In precisely similar fashion one can imagine a rich resident of Eaton Square or its environs in London today being 'hazy' about what it was that Christians believed or got up to, beyond the knowledge that they rang a bell rather early in the morning. And when one questioned him as to why the bell was rung, would there not be some misty notion that it had to do with 'communion'?

The ignorance of well-disposed persons about Christian beliefs and practices regarding Holy Communion is quite as great now as in the days of the Emperor Trajan. A clergyman friend of mine was once profoundly shocked at a 'civic' service held in a cathedral town. For some reason it was thought appropriate (perhaps it was the enthronement of a bishop) to put the ceremony, to use the modern jargon, 'in the context of the eucharist'. My friend, an old-fashioned high churchman advanced upon the wife of the Lord Mayor and stared with horror at her gloved hands. Was she expecting him to place the Body of Christ on to these? Looking up with an obliging smile, she helped him out of his difficulties: 'Oh, no thank you vicar. We've had the biscuit. We are just waiting for the wine'.

No silent kneeling here before the ultimate mystery; but if the Christian church squanders its sacramental gifts and diminishes their unique importance by 'dishing out' Holy Communion on every possible occasion without instruction or explanation, what does it expect?

The fact, however, remains of its *being* there. And even if the 'world', like Pliny or the Lady Mayoress, has only the dimmest notion of what is involved, they are aware of it: a permanent and true sign to our world. Between the time of the emperor Trajan and our own, the action has been repeated and continued. Doubtless it has often been done unworthily. Perhaps it has always been done unworthily. The wordings of the various rites, old and new, have never pretended otherwise. 'We are not worthy so much as to gather up the crumbs under thy table', said the Book of Common Prayer, while in other rites, the faithful spoke the simple Bible words of the centurion, 'Lord I am not worthy that thou shouldest come under my roof'. Nevertheless, it was there. And all over the world, it goes on being there: the bread and the cup offered, which even the stranger to the faith recognises as its distinctive hallmark. I think there is something sufficiently remarkable about the survival of the Holy Communion to merit this perhaps ridiculous labouring of the obvious. Early Christian documents record Jesus as saying to his disciples that he would be with them always, until the consummation of the world (Matthew 28:20). He says he is the true vine, and his followers the branches, who live by not being separated from him. (John

15:1–10). Succeeding generations of Christians have found meaning in his words not on the purely mystical level of interior prayer, but on the sacramental level also. It might be said, and probably rightly, that the sacrament was itself mystical. Of course it is. But it is also visible and practical. It is in approaching an actual altar, an actual priest, an actual patten, an actual Host that we sing the eucharistic hymns which are expressive of this.

> Bread of heaven, on thee we feed,
> For thy flesh is meat indeed.
> Ever may our souls be fed
> With this true and living Bread.
> Day by day with strength supplied
> Through the life of him who died.

Whatever their mood, and whatever their way of expressing their beliefs, and whatever their extent of religious experience or spiritual advancement, those who receive Holy Communion can feel reasonable certainty that they are doing something which stretches back beyond the time of Trajan, back to the time of Paul, back to Jesus himself. Nor, though the external features of the rite – its language, its rituals – may have changed dramatically over the years, can we believe that it has changed in its essence.

*

Earlier, speaking of my own doubts and difficulties, I admitted to being disconcerted by the fourth of the Thirty-Nine articles, which asserts that 'Christ did truly rise again from death, and took again his body, with flesh, bones and all things appertaining to the perfection of Man's nature; wherewith he ascended into Heaven. . . .'

Many people, Christians as well as non-Christians, would say that no one who failed to assent to this proposition could properly be described as a Christian. After all, they would say, either you believe in the Resurrection of Christ or you don't. Either you believe that he rose in the flesh, or you don't. And if he rose in the flesh, what do you suppose happened to his body? It ascended into heaven, of course. This style of argument is helpful to some people, as I have discovered when expressing my doubts about any person with a modern perception of the cosmos being able to absorb Saint Luke's account of Jesus's ascension, in the *Acts*. 'When he had said this, they saw him lifted up, and a cloud caught him away from their sight'. (Acts 1:9). It would perhaps be foolish, as well as profane, to dwell upon this story were it not for the fact that many people, finding it impossible to believe, have felt morally obliged to describe themselves as 'agnostics' and to think that they did not after all 'believe in Christianity'.

None of the other evangelists tell us, however, that Jesus was removed from this earth like an American sky-rocket, and even Saint Luke, in his Gospel, as opposed to *Acts*, tells us in his other version of the Ascension story that 'he lifted up his hands and blessed them; and even as he blessed them he parted from them, and was carried up into heaven'. (Luke 24:51) a phrase with less disturbingly aeronautic detail than the expanded version in the *Acts*.

Saint Paul says that the whole Gospel would collapse if we were unable to believe that Jesus Christ had risen from the dead, destroyed death and brought to the human race the possibility of everlasting life beyond the grave; he warns the Corinthians not to speculate upon the exact nature of the Resurrection body. (I Corinthians 15, 35 etc.). But he has assured them (writing perhaps twenty-five years after the event?) that the Risen Lord was seen 'by more than five hundred of the brethren at once, most of whom are alive at this day'. (I Corinthians 15:6).

This text alone must have reassured many believers, but it has done nothing to shake the unwavering unbelief of the theologians who find the resurrection of Christ completely impossible to believe. For my part, I do not see how one *can* be a Christian if one does not believe Christ rose from the dead, and that in an objective and absolute sense. I have often heard clergymen say that Christ did not rise from the dead, but that it made sense (often 'a very real sense') to speak of him being 'alive' in the hearts and minds of his disciples. This does not make sense to me. I would rather a dead Christ of beloved memory than one who was merely alive in 'a very real sense' which obviated any need to believe in his resurrection.

'Blessed are those who have not seen, and yet have learned to believe', (John 20:29), says the risen Christ to Doubting Thomas. Thomas was asked if he would not thrust his hands into the very wounds of the glorified Jesus. Shamed and crumpled, he can only reply, 'My lord and my God'. (John 20:28). Other doubting Thomases at later stages of history would like to have had his opportunity to discard ocular evidence in favour of blind faith. But we don't have ocular proof, or any other proof. We are not the contemporaries of over five hundred brethren who have seen the Risen Jesus in the flesh. Perhaps, being the contemporaries of five hundred Egyptians who have seen the Blessed Virgin hovering over the rooftops of suburban Cairo – as I gather that we are – we should not be much impressed anyway by eye witness reports of the resurrection appearances.

To be Christian, a person must believe, or come to believe, that Jesus broke the bonds of death and rose from the tomb. I do not think that this obliges anyone to have a particular theory about *how* the resurrection happened. Nor do I think it is even necessary to have a lot of elaborate theories about the historicity of the Gospels, the extent to which they doctored or touched up the evidence. It would seem that to believe in the resurrection is to accept an apparently incredible story as a piece of historical fact. But it is only a purely historical fact, or rather a purely historical fiction, for those who do *not* believe it. Of course, the Christian must accept that there was an empty tomb, and that this was not the result of mere trickery or body-snatching. But a belief in the resurrection is not solely a matter of deciding whether one trusts the five hundred witnesses, or the stories in the Gospels. For it must entail the trust, and it might even lead on to the certainty, that Jesus is alive today.

It is for this reason that I have chosen to discuss the Resurrection in the chapter about Holy Communion. The

Sacrament, as an historical fact, has been going on ever since the death of Jesus. 'It is the Lord's death that you are heralding, whenever you eat this bread and drink this cup', Saint Paul told the Corinthians (I Corinthians 11:26). It would be puzzling if they wished to go on heralding the Lord's death had the ignominious and shameful end to the story been on the hill of Golgotha and not in the Garden of the Resurrection. On the other hand, human beings are puzzling, never more so than when expressing religious certainties. There is no proof. Only faith. But among the faithful, for very nearly the last two thousand years, there has been a belief that the risen Lord Jesus is not to be found in visions, or dreams, nor even in the pious anecdotes of evangelists and apostles who were witnesses to the strange events out of which Christianity dawned. The experience of Christians, the belief that Jesus was alive and present in the world, has been sustained over the centuries, discovered, lost, and rediscovered in the belief that Jesus was truly present in the breaking of bread.

And it was Saint Luke who (for all his troubling accounts of Jesus rising into the clouds) wrote what Renan condescendingly called 'the most beautiful book in the world', and who gives in narrative version the most pregnant account of the Christian experience of the Eucharist. On the very third day on which the empty tomb was discovered, the mother of Jesus had been to the apostles, together with her female companions, and told them of the resurrection. Her story was rejected as 'madness, and they could not believe it'. (Luke 24:11).

Meanwhile, two disciples walked off to Emmaus, discussing all that had happened. A stranger approached and asked what it was that was so absorbing their conversation. 'And one of them, who was called Cleophas, answered him, What, art thou the only pilgrim in Jerusalem who hast not heard of what has happened there in the last few days?' (Luke 24:18). They tell him the whole pathetic story, their hopes that Jesus had been the man who was 'to deliver Israel' (from the Romans presumably), the arrest, trial and execution of their beloved hero, and now, worst of all, the body snatched away from the tomb, and the womenfolk creating an hysterical disturbance by some story of angels appearing before them. The pilgrim expresses amazement at their stupidity and lack of imagination (Luke 24:25), and expounds through all the Scriptures the doctrine that Jesus had been the fulfilment of the old Jewish prophecies, the perfecting of the law. When they reach their destination, the stranger makes as if to go further, but they beg him to stay for it is already getting late.

> So he went in to stay with them. And then, when he sat down at table with them, he took bread, and blessed, and broke it, and offered it to them; whereupon their eyes were opened and they recognised him; and with that, he disappeared from their sight.

> (Luke 24:30–32)

Saint Luke is addressing an audience, as Saint John was when he told the story of Doubting Thomas, who had not seen, but yet had believed. Luke's story could be echoed in the testimony of innumerable Christians since. They did not recognise the risen Lord as he walked with them by the roadside. They did not particularly understand his words, though as he did so, their hearts were burning within them. It was only afterwards that the significance of what had happened dawned. In the morning of the first Easter, the women who went to the tomb were asked, 'Why are you seeking one who is alive, here among the dead?' (Luke 24:5). In the evening, two men had walked with that One who was alive, but they had still not seen who he was. For if the grave was no place to seek him, nor was the roadside where his glorified and risen body walked unrecognised. The risen Christ was perceived when he performed the action that, four days earlier, he had instructed his apostles to repeat. 'They recognized him when he broke bread' (Luke 24:35). The mystery has been repeated, unfolded, enlarged and sustained at every Christian altar since. The Christian's experience of Jesus in Holy Communion is inseparable from the Christian's experience of the Resurrection. His faith in one grows out of his faith in the

71

other. But in this extraordinary sign, the believer does not strain after proofs or weigh evidence. The experience is found in receptivity. It is not something made with the mind or grasped with the intellect. It is something received, and, as at Emmaus, not understood.

'You must sit down', says Love, 'and taste my meat'.
So I did sit and eat.

CHAPTER FIVE

The Upper Room

In St John's gospel, Jesus speaks of himself as the bread of life. 'Your fathers who ate manna in the desert, died none the less; the bread which comes down from heaven is such that he who eats of it never dies'. (John 6:49–50). But the heavenly bread in which Jesus gives himself to the world in the Holy Communion differs also from the manna in the wilderness, in that it is not showered down from the clouds to feed anyone who will partake of it. The Holy Communion is dispensed through human means, by a man standing at an altar, saying the words that Jesus said. That is how it is. If we wish to obey the commands of Jesus, to eat his flesh and drink his blood (John 6:55, 56), we must go to church; and, not merely go to church but belong to a church, or the church.

One immediately encounters a bewildering range of choice, if one lives in an English town. And as I have described the matter, I have made the holy sacrament seem as if it were a commodity. If we were in search of a commodity, we might very well shop around until we found what suited us. But receiving Holy Communion is not an experience of that kind. Christians have always believed that in Holy Communion they receive Jesus himself. The figure before them in the strange clothes is a clergyman, but in so far as he is a priest he is merely dispensing Christ's priesthood. The elements set forth have all the appearance of bread and wine. But this is no ordinary meal. For like the disciples at Emmaus, Christian people believe that they encounter Jesus himself in that breaking of bread. Part of the significance of the action is that when we kneel before the altar, we do so in a company of people who have been together round that holy table since the day when Jesus himself first offered bread and wine in an upper room at Jerusalem. We kneel here in a particular church on a particular Sunday. In the same church ten years ago, a group of people were doing the same, and eating the same heavenly food. Some of them are still here today. Some have gone away. Some are dead. Go back twenty years, and the continuity is unbroken: twenty-five years, two hundred years, close on two thousand.

It was this idea of direct historical continuity with the times of Jesus which led me in my late teens to embrace Catholicism. Jesus instituted the Eucharist. And there was one institution on earth who had kept up that holy offering in an unbroken pattern ever since. The pattern and shape of that offering had changed and become formalised, as one would expect with a human institution. The language of the liturgy, after the conversion of the Roman Empire, became that of the imperial power, so that in a very palpable and perceptible way, this mystery was the same mystery which had been celebrated in the Dark Ages. People speak of the Tridentine Mass as though the bulk of that liturgy were composed during the Council of Trent, and was therefore of not much greater antiquity than the English Prayer Book. But in fact, in substance, the old mass was the same as that used by Alcuin during the reign of Charlemagne. Antiquity is not everything. Universality is not everything. But what that stupendous thing the old Latin mass proclaimed to the world was the unchanging eucharistic presence of Jesus Christ, 'the same, yesterday, today and forever'. It was not a mere matter of convenience that you could go to mass in Tokyo, Tottenham or Toronto and witness the same miracle in exactly the same form, and framed in exactly the same words. It was a sign of Christ himself. It was a sign that Christians did not merely believe in Jesus's coming to our heart as an emotional experience; but rather that they believed his coming to the world, the real, recognisable, human, materialist world, and his remaining in it, to be a matter of historical fact. Much has therefore been lost since the abandonment of that liturgy in the church of the West. Many Catholics remain baffled at the wholesale vandalism which allowed it to be swept away as if it had never been. Of course, the mass remained, Holy Communion remained, in essence unchanged. But the sign of antiquity and of unity with Jesus Christ, which the older rite represented, has been lost forever to the human race.

It might follow from all this that I was also converted to a hard line view that salvation outside the Roman Church was impossible. But this was not so. At the time, I was under the impression that I knew a lot of church history, and I thought that the Catholic view was unanswerable. If Jesus founded a church, it must follow that this church was the One Holy Roman and Catholic Church. The history of the Church of England starts with Henry VIII. The history of the Methodist Church starts with John Wesley. There is only one church whose history starts with Jesus Christ, and that is the Church of Rome. I furthermore felt much more confident than I do now that Saint Peter was the first bishop of Rome, and that it was of the Roman Catholic Church that Jesus was speaking when he declared, 'Thou art Peter and it is upon this rock that I will build my church'. (Matthew 16:18).

If I was so certain, how did I come to leave the Church of Rome and find myself back in the chaotic old national church, founded by Henry VIII? I am not a particularly rational person, and I am easily swayed by my emotions. I was marrying an Anglican who did not, as I have already mentioned, wish to make the necessary promises for marriage in the Roman Catholic Church. I was, besides, deeply homesick for the Church of England: for its buildings, its music, its liturgy, its variety, its tolerance. I took advice. One Catholic priest said to me, 'I don't think you ever *left* the Church of England' – he regarded me as such a hopelessly sentimental Betjeman-style Anglican. Another, a monk who had left the C of E thirty years before said to me, '*Extra ecclesiam nulla salus*: outside the church there is no salvation. It was that which brought me into the church. But I have discovered the truth of its corollary. *Ubi salus, ibi ecclesia* – where salvation is, there the

Church must be also'. So, in rather a chaotic manner, I started to worship once more in Anglican churches, though the vicar of the church where I was married considered it completely unnecessary to be 'received into' the Church of England. He thought there was but one 'upper room' and it did not matter whether you called it Rome or Canterbury. When one saw the inside of his 'upper room' it was not surprising that this pleasant confusion existed in his mind, since it was more crammed with relics, incense-smoke, statues of Our Lady and holy water stoups than any church of the Roman obedience in the town where I was living. Moreover the liturgy he used at my nuptial mass was word for word identical to the beautiful old rite which some call Tridentine.

Doubtless there is an element of play-acting and fantasy in the extreme Anglo-Catholic position, and I would not pretend that I arrived at it by purely logical means. Since those days, I think I have become less of a 'spike' and settled down to more recognisably Anglican modes of worship. Conservative Catholic friends believe that I have apostasised and pray for my reconversion, and every so often, an aspect of the Church of England strikes me as so ludicrous or repellent that I start in terror and think I must 'go back'. But in the Christian life, there is never really any going back, I am happy to say, and because accident has placed me in this particular corner of the Upper Room, I can view it with my own particular perspectives. Indeed, I have gone into such autobiographical detail precisely for that reason. For the 'church' is not an abstract thing. It is a particular organisation, now unfortunately labelled C of E, United Reformed, Roman Catholic, Orthodox and so on. If I had been a 'cradle Catholic' my perspective, naturally would have been different. If I were a happy member of the Baptists whose mind had never been led in the particular direction of considering the historical claims of Catholicism, once again, my view would be different. I can only speak as I am, and from where I am. I have absolutely no qualifications to speak of the matter as a scholar.

At about the time that the monk said to me, 'Where salvation is, there the church is', I happened to attend a Roman

Catholic mass which for some reason was held in an Anglican monastery. The Blessed Sacrament was reserved on the altar, and the Roman clergyman, before starting the service (it was, I seem to recall a 'quiet day') removed the Sacrament from the Tabernacle, and replaced it with his *own* sacrament. When I asked him about this, he said that he himself was perfectly prepared to believe that Jesus was present in the Anglican as in the Roman sacrament, but that he had put a sacred host consecrated by himself into the Tabernacle to satisfy the tender consciences of those Catholics present who did *not* believe. It shows how much I was still an Anglican at heart. This behaviour struck me as extraordinary. I said so to a friend of mine who was present, and she surprised me by saying that she was very glad that the two Hosts had been substituted, for she did actually believe Jesus to be present in one and probably absent from the other.

I mean no disrespect at all to Catholics by including this story. I mention it, trivial as it is, because it helped me to focus my mind on what I believed about the Upper Room. About the same time I got to know the writings of Father Andrew SDC, an Anglican religious who is chiefly remembered today for his letters of spiritual counsel, and for the fact that he was the spiritual director of the founder of the Old Vic, Lilian Bayliss. 'To one thinking of joining the Roman Communion', he wrote,

In approaching this matter the whole point really is, what kind of God do you believe in? When a priest goes to the altar, is it a case of the priest using God to bring the Sacrament to the altar, or God using the priest to give His Sacrament to the people? Do you believe in the kind of God Who would allow England to be separated from Him sacramentally, or do you believe in the kind of God Who, for all the faults of the Church, has none the less kept His vital link with those for whom he was content to die upon the Cross? Do you believe in the kind of God Who is saying to Himself, 'I wish Father Andrew would lose faith in his orders. I wish the whole body of the Church of England,

Australia, South Africa, the whole Anglican Communion, would stand up and own that their bishops are not bishops, that they have never been confirmed or received a true sacrament and would all begin to prepare for Confirmation? Ask yourself, would that be the holy will of an all-wise God? To my mind, it would be not a providence but a muddle.

It is not my purpose to wonder how many English Roman Catholics do or do not believe in that kind of a God. (Very few I would guess.) All I knew when I first read those words was that I did not. The Sacrament was the Sacrament of Jesus Christ, and not the Sacrament of Rome or Canterbury. All Christians share a common, Catholic, baptism. They are not baptised into the Methodist Church or the Church of England or the Church of South India, they are baptised into the Catholic Church of Christ. To that extent, the unity of Christ's Church can not be broken. Similarly, the Holy Communion is the gift of Jesus Christ himself to his people. I believe in the kind of God who uses the priest 'to give his sacrament to his people'. That is the true Catholic doctrine. If I am asked, 'Do you also believe that Jesus Christ is present in the Methodist Sacrament or the Baptist Sacrament or the Presbyterian Sacrament, in the same way that he is present in the Catholic or the Anglican Sacrament?', I would say that it was none of my business to pronounce an opinion. But where Jesus is, there the church is.

The Church of England is in a peculiar position. Cut off from Rome by purely political circumstances, she was established as a national church with only the haziest *theological* foundation. Most other Protestant churches broke with the Pope for theological and religious reasons. Although these elements were not absent in the case of the English church, no one can say that the break occurred because of Transubstantiation, or Justification by Faith alone or all the curious issues which appeared so to possess the sixteenth century mind. I am no historian and no theologian. But I have spoken to many who are and I have never met one professional historian who believed that the Church of England abandoned any of the essential ingredients of the Catholic religion when it made the break. It kept the Catholic orders of bishop, priest and deacon (even though these are less ancient than Christianity and do not stretch back to apostolic times); it kept the notional possibility of seven sacraments and the practice of at least two. It absorbed, of course, much of the new Protestant teaching.

But I have never heard it suggested recently, as used to be often said, that Archbishop Parker, the first Protestant Archbishop of Canterbury (or rather non-Roman archbishop) was consecrated in a manner any less 'valid' than his continental counterparts. One is at liberty to believe, with Thomas More, that it is unlawful for a church to separate itself from the vicar of Christ. More died for this belief, refusing to accept the idea that a king could be governor or 'head' of a church. One is at liberty to believe that the Roman see has, throughout history, protected the Church from false doctrine, heresy and schism. But it does not mean that those who have, by accident, inherited a church created by that sin of schism, do not receive the sacraments of Jesus Christ. In so far as anyone receives Jesus Christ in his sacraments, they surely are already in that one upper room in which the rather absurd denominational differences of Christendom cannot be mentioned without blasphemy. When I say, with trepidation, in the Creed that I believe in One Holy Catholic and Apostolic Church, I mean that I believe in the Sacraments – one baptism for the remission of sins, one bread, one body. I regret the divisions in Christendom, but considering the way in which Christians have behaved in the past, I regard them as inevitable. Of course there is only one church founded by Jesus Christ (if it makes sense to speak of him 'founding a church'). It is perhaps more helpful to think of Jesus merely instituting the Eucharist, and to regard the existence of a 'Church' as a necessary consequence of this fact. I nearly wrote 'a necessary evil'. But the 'Church' has produced many saints; and the 'Church' preserved for us, through all the difficult years of its early persecutions, its obscurities, its internal dissensions, the Gospel or Good News of Jesus Christ. Without the Church, there would be no Gospel and no Sacraments. I do not say that there would be no saints, but there would perhaps have been fewer saints.

By the Church, I mean the ancient and apostolic church as it has come my way, surviving in all its cumbrous, elephantine though divided form in the Catholic West. The Eastern Church has performed a similar, and in modern times almost more remarkable task in countries where it is indigenous. It of course is just as ancient as the Church of Rome and shares common roots. But I am thinking of the Church as it has impinged upon me, and on my country and my continent. I would not wish to deny that in some sense or another Henry VIII 'founded' the Church of England, and Wesley the Methodists, and so on, whereas the Catholic Church was 'founded' by Jesus Christ. But I would say that there was no need to think or speak of 'the Church' in this way. In so far as they all share in the Baptism of Jesus Christ, the Anglicans and the Methodists are as much part of the Church Christ founded as the Roman Catholics. It was not the Church of *Rome* which he founded, it was the Catholic Church. To a certain extent this thing, the Catholic Church, is a thing which exists for all to see. In other ways it is only an ideal after which all Christians aspire. 'Strengthen in faith and love' says one of the prayers in the new Mass, 'your pilgrim church on earth'. Michael Ramsey the former Archbishop of Canterbury is said to have written, 'I believe in the Holy Catholic Church and sincerely regret that it does not exist'. 'That is to say', an old Roman priest said to me sorrowfully, 'that Lord Ramsey believes that the promises of Christ have failed'. It could mean, however, that there were certain promises which it was wrong to suppose Christ to have made in the first place. If we believe that we can be born into Christ by baptism, and fed by Christ in Holy Communion, how can we say that his promises have failed? What greater promise, on this side of the grave, could be offered to us?

★

The Church's function is to mediate Jesus Christ to the world. It was the 'church', the gathering together of the faithful, who gave to the world the Scriptures. It is the church which has preserved the apostolic ministry whereby Jesus Christ promised 'authority' to the Twelve. Authority to baptize in his name (Matthew 28:19), and to pronounce, in his name, the forgiveness of sin (Matthew 16:9). All this necessarily involves church *order*, which has differed greatly from generation to generation and from country to country. But in all these things, I find it necessary to remind myself of Father Andrew's distinction: 'When a priest goes to the altar is it a case of the priest using God to bring the Sacrament to the altar, or God using the priest to give his sacrament to the people?' The Church is Jesus Christ's, but Jesus Christ does not belong to the Church. He is not the church's property.

It is in this connexion that one should recall some other ways of thinking about the Church as well as its sacramental function. I remember once in Italy seeing, at the back of a church, a slot machine which contained communion wafers. those who wished to receive the holy sacrament were asked to put a coin in the slot, and receive a wafer which they were then asked to place in a basket. The basket would be carried to the altar at the moment of consecration. This arrangement was lost on many visitors to the church who, I recall, were plainly under the impression that the machine dispensed *consecrated* hosts, thus cutting out the necessity of hearing mass at all.

The Catholic Church is more than a slot-machine for dishing out sacraments to 'the faithful'. It *is* the faithful. The Prayer Book reminds us that receiving the Holy Sacrament is an assurance 'that we are very members incorporate in the mystical body of thy Son, which is the blessed company of all faithful people'. And the new rite says, 'From age to age you gather a people to yourself so that from east to west a perfect offering may be made to the glory of your name'. It is these *people* who are not merely fed by the body of Christ. They are the body of Christ, 'organs of it depending upon each other'. (I Corinthians 12:27). 'On him all the body depends; it is organised and unified by each contact with the source which supplies it;' (Ephesians 4:16).

In the last discourses of Christ in Saint John's Gospel, he tells the apostles that he is going away from them, but that he will ask the Father to send 'another to befriend you, one who is to dwell continually with you forever. It is the Truth-giving Spirit'. (John 14:16). It was clearly part of John's belief that the gathering-together of the faithful who 'do not belong to the world' (John 17:16), had been given this Spirit. He depicts the disciples locked in the Upper Room on that first day of the week when Mary Magdalen had her encounter in the Garden of the Resurrection with one she supposed to be a gardener. (John 20:15). The same evening, he came to the Upper Room.

> Once more Jesus said to them, Peace be upon you; I came upon an errand from my Father, and now I am sending you out in my turn. With that, he breathed on them, and said to them, Receive the Holy Spirit; when you forgive men's sins, they are forgiven, when you hold them bound, they are held bound.

> (John 20:21)

John compresses into the space of a few hours what Luke depicts as the happening of several weeks – the discovery of the Resurrection, the return of Jesus to His father, the giving to the disciples of the Holy Ghost. Clearly, it only makes a limited amount of sense to talk about these happenings chronologically at all. The coming of Jesus into the world – however it is interpreted theologically – is an attested historical fact. The giving of the Eucharist, the Passion of Christ, and his death are events rooted in history. The descent of the Holy Spirit is an event of the Church's inner life. From the day of Pentecost – which is when Saint Luke, in the *Acts*, 'dates' the descent of the Holy Spirit, many Christians 'date' the origin of the Church. They call it 'the Church's birthday'. It is easy enough to see why they do this. But although, after the first arrival of the Holy Spirit, the behaviour of the Apostles struck the inhabitants of Jerusalem as drunken and hysterical (Acts 2:13), one can not speak of the descent of the Holy Spirit as an historical 'event' in the same way that one can speak of the life of Jesus. The latter can be attested by external means and recognised by non-believers as well as believers. The former, the coming of the Spirit, is something which only the believer can recognise.

The doctrine of the Holy Spirit is therefore one which serves to emphasise the *difference* between the Church and the world. One sees this tendency in the modern church most vigorously. There are two sorts of Christian who are most anxious to claim that they have been visited by the Holy Spirit. Violently different in temper, they arrive at highly similar positions of superiority to the rest of the world. The first sort which springs to mind is the Christian who believes himself to have 'received the Spirit' in an ecstatic or 'pentecostal' experience. Perhaps he speaks with tongues. Perhaps he shakes. Perhaps he performs divine healing. Perhaps he is gifted with some form of enthusiastic utterance. I would not wish to deny that these experiences have much in common with very similar phenomena in the New Testament. And who is anyone to say whether they are 'genuine' or not? The harvest of the spirit, the Galatians were told, is one 'of love, joy, peace, patience, kindness, generosity, forbearance, gentleness, faith, courtesy, temperateness, purity'. (Galatians 5:22). Where these elements are present in the 'pentecostalist', who could complain? But there are some Christians who ask, 'Have you received the Spirit?' in an accusatory rather than evangelical tone. There are some Christians who believe that without the 'baptism of the Holy Spirit' you can not be a proper Christian, and that those who are temperamentally or intellectually ill-equipped to absorb the pentecostalist mode are at best second-class citizens in the Kingdom. The gift of the Spirit comes to such people as a narrowing down, a calling to greater exclusivity even than is provided by the boundaries of what we call the Church.

There is another type of Christian with a particular devotion to the Holy Spirit; not to the Spirit who inspires the Church with ecstatic utterance or the gift of tongues, but to the Spirit who comes 'to guide you into all truth'. (John 16:13). This

Holy Spirit is at work 'protecting' the Church from 'error'. He is believed to be at work all the time, but he is apparently especially at work on certain specified occasions: during the various councils of the Church, for instance, when the fathers debated the Creeds and the evolution of the Faith. During the past one hundred and ten years, moreover, the Holy Spirit has chosen an even narrower field for his protective operation, by governing the mind of the Vicar of Christ, who, since July 1870 has been guarded by the Holy Spirit from making errors when he speaks on matters of faith or morals or doctrine from a particular piece of furniture in the Vatican.

In both cases, that of the pentecostalist and the ultra-papalist, there is a desire to see the field of the Holy Ghost's operation as negative and narrowing. In both cases, it appears, at first to be a positive thing: the bubbling joy of the pente-costal experience, or the wonderfully inspiring belief that the Holy Spirit is so intimately present in the Church that He will protect it from making any fundamental theological error. When I think of either of these extremes in religion, however, I feel rather happy after all to have been washed, by accident, on the shores of a church which happily admits that the General Councils of Christendom 'may err and sometimes have erred, even in things pertaining unto God' (Article XXI), and which, a little belligerently perhaps, asserts that 'as the Church of Jerusalem, Alexandria and Antioch have erred; so also the Church of Rome hath erred, not only in their living and manner of Ceremonies, but also in matters of Faith'. (Article XIX).

I do not believe that human beings *can* be protected from error, any more than they can be protected from sin. I do not believe that there is any Christian reason for supposing that they are. The Church does right to pray and hope that she is guided by the Holy Spirit and that she has been given the gift of the Holy Spirit, but wrong to think that she therefore possesses the Holy Spirit. 'The pretending to gifts of the Holy Ghost is a horrid thing, a very horrid thing'. It is the Church which is the possession of the Holy Spirit and not the other way about, just as she belongs to Jesus Christ and not the other

84

way about. Much of the false teaching concerning the church comes about because people, believing the church to be the vessel of the Holy Spirit, must revere her almost as if she were God, as though She alone can bring us Jesus Christ, She alone can bring us the Holy Spirit. That is false. The most that a Catholic should be required to believe is that God made his new covenant with the world through Jesus: that this covenant was renewed and sustained in each succeeding generation through the apostolic order of the church, through the eucharistic offering, through the inspiration of the Holy Spirit. But just as Jesus, in Christian belief, is a sign to the world of what all human beings, made perfect, could become; so, the Church, the baptised company of the faithful, is a sign in microcosm of the human race as a whole. Saint Luke's story of 'the Church's birthday' brings this very vividly to life. For all the Jews gathered into Jerusalem for the Feast of Pentecost are completely astonished when the Apostles burst out of the Upper Room and jabber with 'tongues'.

> Are they not all Galileans speaking? they asked. How is it that each of us hears them talking his own native tongue? There are Parthians among us, and Medes, and Elamites; our homes are in Mesopotamia, or Judaea, or Cappadocia; in Pontus, or Asia, Phrygia or Pamphylia, Egypt or the parts of Libya round Cyrene; some of us are visitors from Rome, some of us are Jews and others proselytes; there are Cretans among us too and Arabians; and each has been hearing them tell of God's wonders in his own language.
>
> (Acts 2:7–11)

Saint Luke provides us with a reversal of the story in the early Chapters of the Book of Genesis about the Tower of Babel, in which God had frustrated the building by confusing the people and making them speak *different* languages. The old fable of the Tower of Confusion (that is what Babel means) is emblematic of the Church. For in so far as the Church is a Tower which people think they can build on their own as a bridge between

Man and God, it is doomed to become a Tower of Confusion. In each generation, the Tower of Confusion is rebuilt; and in each generation, in one way or another, God pours out his spirit on a revivified Church. So Christians believe. But it is foolish of Christians to think that they possess the gift of this spirit. It is He who possesses them.

None of us will ever know why some people are 'religious' and others not; why some nations were converted to Christianity, while others were resistant to it; why, among those nations and those Christians, some have very different experiences of God, and highly various theological beliefs. In so far as Christians are baptised into a new life in Christ, and feed on him in Holy Communion, they have been marked out from the rest of the human race. They are called to be apart, for their lives are now hidden with Christ in God. (Colossians 3:3). It is very easy for them at this point to believe that the Christians are the only ones in whom God is interested; or that the elect are the only ones who are going to be saved; or that all that matters in this world is to be able to subscribe to the Christian orthodoxies. They do not see that though they do know him who is the Way, the Truth, and the Life, they have only been called to do so by him, for his own purposes. The divine society of the baptised is always an imperfect, uncatholic thing in so far as it fails to contain every member of the human race. The chief of the Apostles on the Feast of Pentecost made his first utterance to the inhabitants of Jerusalem in these terms: 'These men are not drunk as you suppose; it is only the third hour of the day. This is what was foretold by the prophet Joel: In the last times, God says, I will pour out my spirit upon all mankind'. (Acts 2:15–17). If Saint Paul was right in his letter to the Romans, the death and resurrection of Jesus was of significance not merely for the Jews, but for the entire human race, those who had been before Jesus, and those who had been born after. It is hard to imagine anything more trivial than the belief that God poured out his spirit on all flesh simply in order to create an exclusive holy club for persons of a particular religious temperament. The Romans were told by Paul that 'the whole of nature, as we know, groans in a common travail'

86

and that 'the Spirit himself intercedes for us, with groans beyond all utterance:' (Rom 8:22, 27). It would be comic, were it not blasphemous, to have reduced these vast religious ideas to the notion that all this had happened so that a small percentage of the human race might receive the sacraments or be spared from error when contemplating the exact constitution of the holy and undivided trinity.

One of the most glorious Christian legends, and one which I think to be more theological than much that passes for 'orthodoxy', is the story of the Harrowing of Hell. It survives only in books which were never included in the New Testament, though a vestige of the story remains in the Apostle's Creed where it is said that Jesus 'descended into hell'. It is a story, in spite of its absence from the official canons of Christian scripture, which has inspired much of the great Christian literature in the world. The souls in hell, the whole condemned human race from Adam to the time of the crucifixion, hear afar off a voice as of a great thundering calling out the Psalmist's words, 'Draw back, O princes, your gates, remove your everlasting doors: Christ the lord the king of glory approacheth to enter in.' Satan is confident that there is no danger, however, for he has brought Jesus to the ultimate ignominy of death on the Cross. Hell, however, tells Satan not to be so confident. He has already rescued Lazarus from their grasp and may well be capable of greater wonders. All the 'saints' – that is, the human race who are dead, listen to the quarrel which is going on between Satan and Hell. And Adam intervenes, saying to Satan, 'O prince of death, wherefore fearest thou and tremblest? Behold the Lord cometh which shall destroy all thy creatures, and thou shalt be taken captive of him and bound'. There is great rejoicing, and in a splendid scene Adam looks about him with some surprise to see how *many* people there are. And he 'marvelled if they were all begotten of him in the world'. A sort of jollification ensues in which some of the 'big names' in Biblical history, from Seth to John the Baptist, identify themselves. But their talk is interrupted again by the great voice outside, bidding Satan open the gates and the King of Glory shall come in. 'Who is the King of

Glory?' Satan and Hell chant back in unison, being answered with the Psalmist's reply, 'The Lord strong and mighty, the Lord mighty in battle'. After this exchange, a man appears with a cross on his back, and knocks, demanding entrance. Since he is a robber, Satan lets him into the house. But the robber is shining and bright, and he has almost no sooner arrived than the voice outside the door is again heard: 'Open thou most foul one, thy gates, that the King of Glory may come in'. And Christ enters, he breaks the gates of hell, he binds Satan in irons, he casts him down into eternal fire, and makes Hell his warder.

> Then the Lord Jesus, the Saviour of all men, pitiful and most gracious, greeted Adam with kindness, saying unto him: Peace be unto thee, Adam, and unto thy children unto everlasting ages. Amen. Then Father Adam cast himself at the Lord's feet, and rose up and kissed his hands, and shed abundant tears, saying: Behold the hands which formed me: testifying unto all. And he said to the Lord: Thou art come, O King of Glory, to set men free and gather them to thine everlasting kingdom. Then our mother Eve also in like manner cast herself at the feet of the Lord, and rose up and kissed his hands, and shed tears abundantly, and said: Behold the hands that fashioned me: testifying unto all.

And so Jesus leads Adam and Eve into Paradise, with the penitent thief who shared his agony on Calvary, and all good men and women who had been born and died in between. Of course, it is only a legend, a myth, one which inspired the church during the Middle Ages, and which could do so again. The point of the myth is obvious. The redeemed are, in fact, the whole human race. The love of Jesus, and the power of Jesus is not even confined by Time. He can descend into the pits of Hell and rescue even those who are long since dead. The all-embracing extent of God's love cannot be comprehended by the human mind, but it is powerfully demonstrated in this old story.

John tells us that Jesus is the Light of the world. 'There is one who enlightens every soul born into the world; he was the true Light. He, through whom the world was made, was in the world, and the world treated him as a stranger'. (John 1:9–11). What applies to Jesus in his earthly history as a man applies also to Jesus in his presence in the world through the Church. His presence is hidden and unrecognised, except to those to whom, for his own reasons, he has chosen to give a glimpse of his glory. He has not made these men and women *better* than any other. He has not revealed himself as fully to them as they would sometimes like, or as they would sometimes pretend. But their calling is to be lights in the world themselves (Matthew 5:14). Jesus is a type and a firstfruit of a new, redeemed humanity, a man for whom God is no longer a stranger, but one who can be addressed intimately as father, and a man who identified himself totally with the poor, the destitute and the outcast. ('I was hungry and you never gave me food' (Matthew 25:42).) To those who 'believe in his name', he gives the opportunity to become 'sons of God' like himself, living in a new relationship with God and the world.

If that is the case, why need there be a distinction between the baptised and the unbaptised? Does Jesus love Christians more than other peoples? There is a difficulty here. A mystery, perhaps more than a difficulty, but one so profound that it has made some of the most thoughtful devotees or friends of Christianity fall, as it were, at the last fence. Simone Weil is the most conspicuous to my mind. She had, not merely a mystical experience of Christ which was so vivid that its reality was unquestionable to her; she had also a profound devotion to Christ in the Sacrament which, as an unbaptized Jewess, she was unable to receive. And she also, in her perverse way, had a very great reverence for the Church. But she would not join it. To the very last, as she lay dying at the age of thirty-four in Kent in 1943, she declined to be baptized. She had no feeling that God wanted her to belong to the Church. Her apostolate was to those outside the church; it was, more fully, on their behalf. To the priest who wanted to baptise her, she wrote:

You can take my word for it . . . that Greece, Egypt, ancient India, and ancient China, the beauty of the world, the pure and authentic reflections of this beauty in art and science, what I have seen of the inner recesses of human hearts where religious belief is unknown, all these things have done as much as the visibly Christian ones to deliver me into Christ's hands as his captive. I think I might even say more. The love of those things which are outside visible Christianity keeps me outside the Church.

It was because the Church was not Catholic that Simone Weil felt unable to join it. She could not submit to baptism if by that she implied that Christ was not also present in the Bhagavad Gita, in Homer, and in the lives of her atheist friends. '. . . in my eyes Christianity is catholic by right but not in fact. So many things are outside it, so many things that I love and do not want to give up, so many things that God loves, otherwise they would not be in existence'. Strangely enough, her gesture of remaining outside the Church has brought many converts to Christ since her death. She was a true saint: like many saints, maddening and arrogant, but also full of God.

There is no doubt that her fastidious refusal to be baptized draws attention to a fundamental paradox about Catholicism. On the one hand, it is necessary to be baptized in order to be 'in Christ'. On the other Christ Himself is bigger than his sacrament. On the one hand Catholics pray 'from age to age you gather a people to yourself'. But they believe that the significance of this gathering-together is that all humanity, and all created things, which have groaned and travailed without God, should be drawn back into communion with him. To narrow this down to a simple desire that all human beings should be Christians is scarcely consistent with believing in a God who 'poured out his spirit on all flesh'. 'In approaching this matter the whole point really is, what kind of God do you believe in?'

Is it the kind of God who has stored up everlasting punishment for those who do not believe in the doctrines of Christianity? Is it the kind of God who believes that there are first class citizens – the ones with baptismal certificates – and second-class, benighted citizens who have not been baptized? Is it the kind of God who can not be found, and can not reveal himself in many different ways, and in many different religions throughout the world, who is so tied down by his presence in the Catholic sacrament or the word of Christian scripture that he fails to inhabit the temple of a sikh, the soul of a Buddhist, the Scriptures of a Moslem?

I am not saying that all religions are one. They plainly are not. I am not saying that there is no distinction between those who have been baptized or heard the Good News of Jesus Christ and those who have not. There plainly is. I am saying that this Good News does not only apply to those who hear it, and the Church is not only a club for those who belong to it. The Church will always be incomplete until all men have found their place laid at the table in the Upper Room. Since the Host in the upper room tells us not to judge other people, we do not know why it should be impossible to take a place there, even though we have not believed as the Church teaches. The Church's calling is to convert the world, and also to serve the world. As the body of Christ, she must like Christ move in the world, especially among the sinners who feel no hope, the sick who need healing, the poor, the naked, the hungry and the imprisoned. Where Christians do this, opening the doors of the upper room and stretching out to Christ's people in the world, we glimpse a little of how the church is *both* the blessed company of all *faithful* people and also the mere first-fruits of the harvest, a mere paradigm of what is to come, at the great Messianic banquet of him who poured out his spirit on *all flesh*.

That is the importance of the Christian doctrine of Heaven. The idea of heaven is not a theory about the after-life which might be sent off to the Society for Psychical Research for comparison with other 'theories' such as non-survival, or the transmigration of souls. The Christian idea of heaven is rooted in the belief that all men are made in God's image and likeness, and that all men are creatures who should know and love God not only in this life but beyond death, too. In so far as they speak of the Church Triumphant, in heaven, Christians recognise the incompleteness of the Church militant here on earth. Nobody knows what will happen beyond the grave. All that the Bible can give us is picture language. The visionary who wrote the Apocalypse speaks of a city which had no need of sun or moon to light it.

> The glory of God shone there, and the Lamb gave it light. The nations will live and move in its radiance; the kings of the earth will bring it their tribute of praise and honour. All day the gates will never be shut (there will be no night there), as the nations flock into it with their honour and their praise.

> (Apocalypse 21:23–27)

Saint Paul does not use picture language in the same way. He speaks instead of the Spirit of God interceding for human beings before they even knew that they ought to pray; of Christ's reconciling power filling the whole of creation, and taking into itself not merely all people, but all flesh, all rocks and stones and trees, all that was made by God at the beginning and found to be 'very good.'

What we call the Church, therefore, the organised body of Christian people on earth, with its various fellow-travellers and sympathisers, can only represent the most tiny proportion of God's purposes and revelation to the human race. The more inward-looking and self-regarding an organisation is, the less it can be the Church. The earthly church can never be complete. It is the presence in this world of One whose Kingdom was not of this world. Its consummation will not be here or now. Its calling is to include, and not exclude the men and women whom God loves.

That, quite incidentally, was one of the very attractive and also very theological virtues of the Church of England when it was conceived of, not as one sect among many, but as the National Church. The parson in his parish was responsible for *everyone* in that parish, whether they came to church or not; and whether or not they expressed allegiance to some other sect or creed. Twice a day he was meant to ring a bell and then read the services of morning and evening prayer. He did not expect the whole town or village to come to these services. He would perhaps be surprised if a single person turned up. But the ringing of the bell signified that he was offering prayer for all who heard it. And the repetition of these services, of matins and evensong, the pure worship and praise of Almighty God, was something which many could attend with devotion who were not yet ready or able to commit themselves wholly to Christ in his sacraments.

The C of E, comic and mundane as it is often made to sound, was actually a more Catholic church, in a sense of being a church of more universal appeal to a wider range of people, than any other church in Western Europe. When I say 'appeal', I do not mean that it was more *attractive*, but that it expressed very fully the diverse degrees of need and sympathy not only of the people who belonged to it, but also of those who did not. Those who looked at its doctrinal positions and found them chaotic or uncohesive; those who looked at its liturgical observances and found them diversely anarchic; those who looked at its position as an established religion and believed it perversely to be rendering unto Caesar things which should properly have been rendered unto God did not perhaps believe that it *was* a Church. They did not understand what a richly spiritual thing it was; nor how its prayer book was more than a literary gem, a great source of religious strength to those who, while calling themselves protestants could absorb all its wealth of Catholic liturgy, prayer and spirituality; or, while calling themselves Catholics, could rejoice in the Reformation free-doms of the Gospel, could soak up its vast biblical lectionary, and use its prayers without any danger of vulgarity or dis-honesty. Was it not a monument of Christian spirituality worth preserving? And was the national church not a beautiful thing, a Christian thing, of unique value, unparalleled in the world?

I speak of it in the past. For, although the Church of England is still by law established, it has changed its nature into that of a sect. Fearful of seeming paternalistic, it has abandoned its claim to be the Christian church in this land, and sought to blend in with all the other denominations in this multi-faith and multi-racial society, as it is called. Those who have made this shift have done so with the best of motives. They have not wanted to 'lord it' over other Christians, and they have felt that in a parish in which there are many Hindus, Sikhs, Moslems and Jews, it would be offensive to say that these people, whatever their religion, were regarded as his flock by the parson. But in fearing to seem bossy, the parsons have abandoned, or are abandoning the potent image of themselves as priests of Christ, who poured out his spirit on all flesh and who said that men would come from the east and from the west to sit down in the Kingdom of Heaven, the great Upper Room. In abandoning a liturgy parts of which were known by heart by enormous numbers of people who never went to church, the parsons have in effect unchurched those people. They have incidentally in so doing destroyed all the echoes of the prayer book which reverberate not only in liturgy but also in popular speech.

Huddled in upper rooms in Corinth and Ephesus, and Rome and Colossae, the first Christians heard a gospel which 'has been preached to all creation under heaven'. (Colossians 1:23). Little could they know that the Catholic church was to become, not only the great civilising force in European history, but also, as it spread and developed, the visibly natural home of the human spirit. 'Within that household, the human spirit has roof and hearth'. (Belloc). Now there is a tendency for the Christians to retreat to their upper rooms once more and to preach a Gospel not to all creation under heaven but to their own select band. But he will not be contained in the upper room. If his promises were true, the church must 'go out, making disciples of all nations' (Matthew 28:19). If one method fails and one form of Christianity fizzles out, he will still go on calling people to himself. The gates of hell will not prevail against it. 'By that I mean the Church of the living God, the pillar and foundation upon which the truth rests'. (I Timothy 3:15).

CHAPTER SIX

The Truth

There is much more to it than I have said. St John ended his
Gospel by saying, 'There is much else besides that Jesus did; if
all of it were put in writing, I do not think the world itself
would contain the books which would have to be written.'
(John 21:25). I have tried to trace very briefly the barest
outlines of what can be said, without dishonesty, about
Christianity. I began with the words of Jesus: his hauntingly
stern paradoxes, his call to poverty, pacifism and chastity; his
assertion that we can only find self by self-denial; life by dying.
I discovered, on reading further in the New Testament, that it
was seemingly the opinion of the early writers that this call to
self-purification was a call to Jesus himself, who came as a
doctor to heal the sick. It was he himself who could forgive us
our sins and enable us to aspire to the counsels of perfection
which fell from his lips. It was in his death that the Gospel
writers, St Paul and the others saw the vindication and
triumph of this claim. The old rites of purifying happened
through the sprinkling of goats and heifers. But it was through
the blood of Jesus that his people were cleansed from their sins.

Christians proclaim the death and resurrection of Jesus
every time they celebrate mass, or the Lord's Supper. They
believe, like the disciples going to Emmaus, that they find the
risen lord in the breaking of bread. This custom, the breaking
of bread, survives through the centuries because of the
Church. Historically, that word Church means the Orthodox
churches of the East and the Latin Church of the West, with all
those occupying an ambiguous position who in varying splin-

ters broke away from Latin Christianity. But that is to speak purely historically, and the New Testament reminds us that the Church is the gathering of all faithful people, united by baptism and guided by the Holy Spirit. This spirit is the Light which lights every man coming into the world, so that, even if it had never been broken by schism, the earthly church could never be complete until it contained all mankind. Its sanctification of bread and wine and feeding them back to the people as the Body and Blood of Christ is emblematic of the whole work of divine grace, which is to sanctify everything in creation.

It is a grand, and a beautiful thing. But is it true? It has sustained thousands and thousands of human lives in the course of its history. It has inspired some of the most heroic acts of virtue, some of the most splendid architecture, some of the most sublime music, some of the most overwhelming paintings. Sometimes, at times of great doubt and confusion, the most I have been able to say as I entered a church was, 'I cannot believe this religion. But I wish to be at one with those who have believed it, and who do. My mind cannot grasp what the great Christians of the past were able to proclaim with such confidence. But at least I can use the words that they used, and kneel in the places where they knelt. For I would rather be at one with them than with the materialism or atheism of my contemporaries'. This attitude of sentimental agnosticism lurks, I suspect, behind much liturgical conservatism. At one with all our pious forebears, we can mouth the very words they mouthed and hear the mass they heard, sustained by their example and prayer, but having only a minimal faith ourselves. Then when the prop of the old words is removed, and the bridge between past and present is broken, we are left not with echoes of the past, but with the creeds and prayer of Christendom laid bare. It may seem amazingly superficial. But the old words can lull us into such a haze of piety that we can readily assent to *et incarnatus est* while suddenly wondering, in the crude modernity of the new text, whether it is possible to believe that 'by the power of the Holy Spirit he became incarnate of the Virgin Mary'. The old liturgies were compiled in the days of faith. When we use their language we are back in an intellectual and moral universe which makes it perfectly possible to talk about God. There is a starker demand made upon our faith when we have to enunciate belief in our own modern idioms; for most people who use those modern idioms do not believe in God, or do not believe in him as our forefathers believed.

If the language of faith is difficult to use nowadays, and if it is admitted that there is a large measure of agnosticism behind apparently conservative Christian attitudes, is there not a sort of heroism in carrying on *as if it were all true*? William Temple said that when a Christian recited the Creed he was saying, 'I undertake to live as if these things were true'. One way of defining faith would be to say that one would go on undertaking so to live even if these things were not true. But if one genuinely thought they were untrue, what then? We might allow that, for a period of doubt or difficulty, it was perfectly proper for a Christian to struggle on with the outward observance of his religion, while inwardly knowing and feeling nothing. All teachers of the spiritual life would seem to suggest that such periods of 'drought' were inevitable. But if, on reasonable reflexion, one found it impossible to believe in God, what then? However much in love one might be, not merely with the outward forms of Christian buildings, liturgy and music, but also with the inner practice of Christian prayer and the aspirations of Christian ethics, would it not be more honest to say that we do not believe in God?

Consider just a few of the difficulties. Biblical scholars have forced Christian apologists into the difficult choice between a retraction of the conventional teaching or a blustering insistence upon things which can not possibly be proved, and which probably are not true. The almost universal belief of Christians, before the findings of Biblical scholarship percolated through, was that the Bible was an inspired book, every word of which was infallibly true. Never mind that it contradicted itself. It was infallibly true. When Bishop Colenso in the 1850s tentatively noted that in the Book of Genesis there were two accounts of Noah's ark, in one of which the patriarch was said to have preserved the species by pairs, in another by sevens, the prelate was summoned back from his colonial see to face a charge of heresy from his fellow-bishops. Mr Gladstone wrote pamphlets asserting that the story of the Garden of Eden was literally and historically true.

But once the Bible had been subjected to the same sort of scrutiny as any other group of ancient texts, certain obvious facts about it emerged. It was, for instance, written by people, each of whom was heavily influenced by the times and society in which he lived. The books of the New Testament were not dispassionate narratives by eye-witnesses. In fact they were not narratives at all, and it could not be denied that the Gospels had been woven together when the Christian tradition was already well-established. Since they were all written by people who believed that Jesus had risen from the dead (but not, in all probability, by the eye-witnesses to those events), that influenced their whole way of telling the stories, and arranging the sayings. The Gospels are as much preaching as St Paul's epistles were.

This dissection of the New Testament by the scholars was not designed to demolish the old Christian creeds, and nor did it have the immediate effect of doing so. But when a scholar assures us that there is no word *parthenos* (virgin) in the language which Mary and Joseph would have spoken (Aramaic) and that, besides, it is only in two of the Gospels that Mary's Virginity is mentioned, what becomes of the doctrine of the Virgin Birth? Sure enough, it is not destroyed by the textual scholars. But they have shown it to be what it is: a piece of church doctrine, and not something for which there is a shred of unbiased historical evidence. From the beginning of the story to the end, the scholars have made it clear that the New Testament is nearly all doctrine, and, although it is rooted in historical circumstances, it is not, strictly speaking, history at all. This does not mean that we have to discard its historical claims. But it makes us look at them more timorously. And in more recent times, timorousness has turned to absolute unbelief.

There is absolutely no proof in the New Testament, for

instance, that Jesus claimed to be God. If one accepts the general premiss of the scholars (and it is very hard not to), there is not a saying in the Synoptic Gospels which an unbiased historian would accept as being a claim by Jesus to be God, or the Second Person of the Trinity. This led a group of New Testament scholars not long ago to write *The Myth of God Incarnate* in which they effectively discarded any suggestion that the Incarnation of Christ was actually and objectively true. There have been several attempts to refute, or to rebuke, these writers; some loud, some panicky, some feeble, some thoughtful. The most profound, and the most effective, is Lord Ramsey's quiet book *Jesus and the Living Past*. He reminds us that most of the arguments in the *Myth of God* book are a revival of old ideas entertained by earlier biblical critics. He reminds us that Saint Paul and the writers of the other epistles never lose touch with the idea of their exalted Christ being one and the same as the earthly historical Jesus. And he also reminds us, a very proper reminder in the middle of what is in danger of being a very arid intellectual debate, that the religion of Jesus is a thing to be lived and experienced if it is to be written about sanely. So we read interlaced with his scholarly reflexions, passages about prayer and about the experience of human suffering.

The question is, however, not whether the *Myth of God* men were wrong about individual interpretations of the New Testament documents, but whether now is not the moment for 'Taking leave of God'. The title is that of a book by the Reverend Don Cupitt, one of the contributors to *The Myth of God Incarnate*, and the author, too, of a subsequent book *The Debate about Christ*. Cupitt has a lively mind which darts about and changes, but the central thesis of *Taking Leave of God* is an attractive one, very similar to ideas propounded, for instance, by Iris Murdoch in her philosophical writings. Very simply, it is this. The chief thing wrong with Christianity is that it proclaims the existence of an externalised unbelievable God. But that is not a reason for abandoning the pursuit of the spiritual life. In fact, once one abandons the crude fiction of an externalised God – the creator of the Universe, the old man in the sky – there is more chance that one can develop a way of spiritual advancement somewhat akin to that of the Buddhists. This, says Cupitt, is less radical than it sounds, for it you examine the actual religious experience of Christians over the centuries you would not find it 'rigidly and uniformly realist'. The practice of Christian prayer is internal. 'The Christian doctrine of God just is Christian spirituality in coded form, for God is a symbol that represents to us everything that spirituality requires of us and promises to us.'

I have paraphrased and quoted at random, but I hope I have not done undue damage to Don Cupitt's argument. In fact, he differs very little, to the layman's eye, from positions that have often been advanced by modern religious philosophers before. It is now thirty years, for instance, since Professor Richard Braithwaite outlined a precisely similar analysis of religious belief and language. He took it for granted that religious statements can not be tested empirically, nor analysed by the standard methods of linguistic philosophy. Religious statements are not like scientific statements which can be checked against some external arbiter. Nor are they *a priori* truths of the sort accepted by mathematicians. In fact, he claimed, 'the intention of a Christian to follow a Christian way of life is not only the criterion for the sincerity of his beliefs, it is the criterion for the meaning of his assertion.' The lecture made clear that Braithwaite did not actually think it necessary for a Christian to believe in God. He asserted that if one accepts a religion (he decided himself to be baptized as a Christian in adult life) what one is doing is accepting a set of 'stories' and saying that one will endeavour to live *as if they are* true.

One has moved from Archbishop Temple's view that the recitation of the Creed means, 'I undertake to live as if these things were true' to the view that this is *all* that the Creed means, or can mean.

It is understandable if philosophers have found it difficult to write about religion since they limited themselves to a set of criteria which condemned as 'meaningless' anything which could not be verified by empirical inquiry. If religion becomes an impossible area of discussion by this standard, so do many of the other interesting areas of life – such as taste, art, the moral life, love and death: all the subjects in fact which laymen regard as the traditional territory of the philosopher. Common sense rebels against the Braithwaite argument. After all, it is possible to imagine someone saying, like a character in a Graham Greene novel, that he believed in a Christian statement but did *not* intend to live as if it were true. 'I sincerely believe that I will be damned if I commit adultery, but I am so much in love that I will do so.' A little melodramatic, perhaps, but a possible sentence? It is also logically possible (though I have never met quite such a person and I find him or her rather hard to imagine) to think of someone who believed in the Resurrection of Jesus but found his teachings so repellent that he felt obliged to reject Christianity. When people say that they do not believe in Christianity they very often do not mean that they intend to behave in an unchristian way. Similarly when men or women say that they *do* believe, that does not prevent them from behaving in a decidedly anti-Christian or immoral way.

It is not simply a matter of behaviour. But if one has reached Don Cupitt's view that God is simply an *internalisation* of our deepest aspirations and longings is one justified in continuing to say the creed and receive the sacraments? I am not, of course, asking this as an intrusive personal question concerning Mr Cupitt's inner life, but as one of general principle. He would say, to judge from *Taking Leave of God* that one was justified because although people in the past thought they believed in a God external to themselves they were really worshipping personifications of religious values which they held close. At an early stage in his thesis, Mr Cupitt has made a boldly disconcerting claim.

Commentators on religious affairs, bemoaning the enfeebled spiritual condition of modern religion, sometimes betray a quite unrealistic and sentimental expectation that modern religious people, if sincere, should have an archaic form of consciousness. Of course they do not. I have met a fair sprinkling of patriarchs, cardinals, bishops, monks and other prominent religious persons and can assure the world that they all have the modern form of consciousness and that not a single one of them believes in God in quite the pre-modern way.

This betrayal of an attitude is disarmingly frank. I can assure you dear reader that everyone *nowadays* is conditioned to think in a particular way, and though you might meet some pious old codgers who say they believe in God, they do not really do so *in the same way* as people used to in the past. Those who do go on believing in the old way are, 'I am sorry to say . . . slightly mad and an object of pity and ridicule'.

It so happened that I read Mr Cupitt's book for the first time during the course of a week in which I also read a volume of Cardinal Hume's essays and sermons, *To Be a Pilgrim*, in which the Cardinal appeared to be enunciating an intelligent but very simple faith in an old fashioned 'belief system'. Lacking Mr Cupitt's advantages, and not having met a sprinkling of Cardinals, I have no way of knowing whether Basil Hume is slightly mad, an object of pity or ridicule, or simply kidding himself that he believes things which he doesn't believe. I quote one short passage from the Cardinal to reveal my difficulty.

Before the tabernacle, I genuflect. Why? Because Christ in the Church tells me he is truly present in the Eucharist. How is he present? That is theology, and the theologians can never fully explain it.

Belief in the reality of Christ's presence in the Blessed Sacrament does not come from reading; it does not come from any man's skill. It comes from faith, from the humility of mind to accept and to say 'yes' to what may seem to be unbelievable, namely that the Body and Blood of Christ are present under the appearances of bread and wine.

Now, I am not entering into the discussion of whether the Cardinal's belief is right or wrong. I am merely noticing that he is expressing a belief in the Real Presence of Christ in the

Eucharist in a form which I can not imagine St Thomas Aquinas finding unexceptionable. Though he admits that it is something which the finite mind can not grasp, that is surely different from saying that the finite mind recognises it is *untrue* but has decided for some reason to behave as if it were true. And it is also different from saying that he has merely internalised a doctrine. On the contrary, he has externalised his belief in a totally incomprehensible article of faith which is based, surely, on the opinion that there is really a God. Cardinal Hume is a more graceful and mannerly man than Hilaire Belloc, but I am reminded of a letter Belloc wrote in which he recalled writing that 'man was never meant to live by his pen'. And Arnold Bennett wrote an angry letter to that newspaper saying, 'What did HB mean by the word "meant"? Meant by whom? Did I (asked Arnold Bennett – a good-natured man with a hare lip and a simple face otherwise) did I mean "meant" by a hypothetical God? To this I answered by yet another letter saying "Yes!" But not "a" (or rather "an") hypothetical God, but by a real God full of beef, creator of Heaven and Earth *et omnium visibilium et invisibilium*'.

Absurd, but surely fair comment? Either there is a God or there isn't. And if there is, he can not be a hypothetical God or an internalised God. He must be a real God. I think of a friend of mine, a member of the Church of England, who for more than twenty years has belonged to an enclosed religious community. She again falls into neither of Mr Cupitt's categories of the 'slightly mad' nor of those who have failed to think of God as somebody completely and objectively real. Her work, like that of her sisters, is prayer, the singing of the divine office, and keeping perpetual watch before the Blessed Sacrament. The sisters do not believe in prayer solely as a form of internal contemplation. They believe in intercessory prayer, prayer for the world, prayer for individual lives and intentions. They may be completely deluded, but it seems to me that they do believe in God 'in quite the pre-modern way'.

I don't actually see how 'modernity' comes into the matter. It is a red herring. If God has an objective and external reality, that reality can not have altered with the passage of the years, since 'his truth endureth from generation to generation'. It is one thing to say that we and our ancestors have a different way of looking at the world; that the degree of our scientific knowledge is infinitely more sophisticated; that this knowledge includes not only our perception of natural phenomena, but also of the human mind and psyche. It is quite another to suggest that anything outside ourselves has thereby changed because of our perceptions. We know much more than Saint Luke did about the construction of the sky. We know more than Saint Paul about what it was like above the clouds. It entitles us to discount their stories and prediction of aerobatics on the part of Our Lord. But it does not entitle us to suppose that clouds and earth were not constituted in the same way in the first century as they are today. The fact that the New Testament writers perceived them differently does not alter the fact of their independent external existence. What holds good for the clouds must, logically, hold good for Jesus himself. What holds for Jesus must hold for God. If he exists, he must always exist. 'Before Abraham was, I am'. The changing perceptions of God, not merely from age to age in the human race, but from day to day in the mind and heart of the believer could not possibly be said to effect God's objective reality, a reality different in kind from those of the clouds and the rocks, but if a reality at all, true and external to ourselves. We can not be said to believe in God if we think he exists purely as an internalisation of our own spiritual aspirations; for that would be to say that God dies when we die. It would appear from Mr Cupitt's book *Taking Leave of God*, as though indeed this does happen. Speaking of the possibility of an after-life, he is able to write, 'There is no such chance. Death is death.'

I am not able to enter into this certainty. To say emphatically that death is death and that there is nothing beyond it, is quite as dogmatic as the old Christian theology which drew an exact map of the after-life. Subscribers to this scheme can tell you – or could (are there any left of this type?) – who was in purgatory, who was in limbo, who ought to be in Hell, and who in Heaven. Since one of the greatest poems in the history of Europe was fashioned out of this way of contemplating death, I would not deprecate it. But it is obviously impossible for an honest rational person to hold as certainties things which must, by definition, be mysteries. I do not feel able to share Don Cupitt's certainty that Plato was wrong, that Mahomet was wrong, that the Buddha was wrong, that almost every European writer from the time of Saint Augustine to the time of Tennyson, was wrong in the belief that human beings did survive death. It is impossible, however, to argue the thing positively. One can only say of death that one does not know. It is the ultimate mystery. And even as we enter into the Christian faith and see that death was a mystery penetrated by Christ, who endured it and returned from it, we still are no nearer explaining it. I would think this was a very important part of our investigation into religious truth. We know that at the end of it, we are going to pass into a mystery. We can not ignore the mystery of it, for it colours our lives. We watch it happen to those we love. We read of it every day; we know that it is happening all around us. It is quite as extraordinary in animals as in human beings. One minute, movement, breath, animation; the next, stillness and emptiness. Is it any wonder that men spoke of a spirit passing out of the body? To see a friend's face in death is to see a mere shell from which the friend has departed. This is a deep mystery, not to be trivialised by assertion, but to be experienced, with awe. It colours all ancient writings about God, and it should colour ours. The choice, when we face death, or when we consider God, is not between ignorance and certitude, but between faith and despair.

Perhaps one of the drawbacks of much religious philosophy in recent times has been the extent to which it assumed that religion was a set of problems, or difficulties, which, if worried at sufficiently, would yield some sort of an answer. At every point, for the lay inquirer, as for the scholar, Christianity resists such lines of approach. Those who have lost faith in it are not necessarily cleverer than anyone else, but they are very often people who have believed it to contain reassurances which were never quite there. It is astonishing to our generation that so many Victorians believed every word of the Bible to be literally and scientifically true. When they discovered that the great myth of creation at the beginning of *Genesis* could not be read as a scientific document, they started to lose their belief in the creative and sustaining power of God in his universe. With no less naivety, many men and women today take no recognition of the fact that the books of the New Testament were penned by particular people, with limited knowledge and specifically evangelical purpose. When they discover that the Gospel according to Saint Luke is not a well-researched modern biography, they start to panic and discard the whole story as 'untrue'.

Meanwhile, the great argument about God revolves in the minds not only of intellectuals and clever people, but of anyone who has witnessed or experienced innocent suffering. God is love, we are told. God is all-powerful. An all powerful God was therefore responsible for the torments of sick children, the wretchedness of famine, the destruction wrought by earthquakes, fire and flood. If he was not 'responsible', how could we say he was all powerful? Viewed this way, it is logically impossible to believe in an all-loving and all-powerful God. Take that together with the fact that one can not regard the Scriptures as infallible, and that there is nothing to prove that we survive death, and the ordinary structure of Christian theology becomes very fragile.

It all purports to be concerned with him who was the Way, the Truth, and the Life. One of the most saintly and ascetic of twentieth century Roman Catholic priests, Father Vincent McNabb OP said that 'Truth alone is worthy of our entire devotion'. And if that is not true then life cascades into pure muddle and nonsense. We *must* be truthful. And does it not follow that if the Christian religion is untrue it must be discarded?

Many truthful people have found, with greater or lesser degrees of regret, that the answer must be *yes*. If one goes through some formulary of Christian belief such as the Apostles Creed with a pencil and ticks each item with which one is or is not in agreement, the average twentieth century mind must often score rather low. And if one faces logical puzzles such as the problem of an all-powerful and all-loving God, one similarly reaches an *impasse*. Add to that the fact that a great deal of biblical 'evidence' now turns out to be non-evidence, or actually false, and one begins to see the attraction of Mr Cupitt's *Taking Leave of God*, For at least that might enable one to retain the spiritual riches of the Christian tradition without dishonesty. The very title, *Taking Leave of God*, comes from the mystic writer Meister Eckhart; and many mystics have worshipped God solely on the interior throne of their own hearts. It is nothing so crude as saying that they were imagining things, but that the religion of the heart has very often recognised God's unknowability, so that there is a short step between the Cloud of Unknowing and the Cloud behind which the modern theologian lurks, the Cloud of Unbelieving.

But this argument won't do, precisely because it is untrue. It is one thing to believe with mystics from Plotinus to the present day, that all we know of God is his unknowability, and to bow before the unknowable mystery. It is quite another to say that we do not believe in God, we do not believe he is *there*, and yet, for some reason of our own, that we are going to continue with the practices of prayer and meditation. The reasons for this are very clear if we return to the mystics themselves. It is only by a very selective reading of their experiences that we can extrapolate a purely internalized religion from even the most neurotically self-centred of them, or even the most blankly negative. The Cloud of Unknowing itself is something which its author wishes to pierce with the burning darts of his love for God.

With similar urgency, the mind and heart of man must be loyal to the truth above all things, for truth alone will save us from fantasy, self-delusion and lunacy. It is not religious to pretend things happened which did not happen; nor to claim that things are the case when they plainly are not. And yet many people have abandoned religion because they thought that this was what religion required and did; and many religious people cling to their old certitudes even though they know them to be untrue. Just as our wills are feeble and we can not follow the Way spelt out in the teachings of Christ, so our minds and imaginations are timorous when confronted with the Truth. Following him who is the Way we discover new approaches not only to our moral dilemmas but also to the revelation of who we are and of the purpose of our lives. Following him who is the Truth we discover that we must not resist our duty to think, but that thought is not the only process by which we experience the Truth. 'Christ likes us to prefer truth to him', Simone Weil wrote, 'because, before being Christ, he is truth. If one turns aside from him to go towards the truth, one will not go far before falling into his arms'.

It is one of the most startling of her sayings. If it is wrong to give assent to things which we know to be false, it is surely equally wrong to shut our minds and hearts to the possibility of being led into an acceptance of things which we do not understand. 'So we read of, Things no eye has seen, no ear has heard, no human heart conceived, the welcome God has prepared for those who love him'. (I Corinthians 2:9). Those of us who believe, and those of us who do not believe, should surely both alike be humble enough to accept the mysterious-ness of divine truth, to accept that there is much that we do not know. *Magna est veritas et praevalebit.*

But this works both ways. Truth in religious life is a positive, not a negative thing. We do not destroy the Truth by discarding untrue things. Rather, we purify our minds and strip them bare for the reception and discovery of truth. That is why, in spite of all the depressing things about modern Christianity, its relentless tendency to be silly, I am glad to be alive now, and to have known all the stimulation and shock of following modern enquiries into religious truth. We know now, thanks to the investigations of textual scholars, that there are many things which our ancestors believed about the Bible which also happened to be false. But at the same time we have been able to read the Bible with fresh eyes and to discover that, if it was written by men with a much more limited knowledge of the world than our own, it nevertheless enshrines truths which are inescapably compelling to us, with our quite different minds and circumstances. We have learnt, similarly, from the philosophers, that many of the assertions and proofs of the older theologians were logically untenable. But we have been released thereby into the discovery that true religion, and faith, only begin when we have abandoned posturing certainty and strident assertion. We have learned much, as we watched the crumbling of institutional Christianity, about the saying that we must die in order to live. For, although many of the beloved old forms of religion have been discarded, religion itself seems bubblingly popular. Many churches are full again. Religious orders which, twenty years ago had started to dwindle, are once more discovering that they are 'getting vocations'. There is a return.

Sobered by the discovery that not all the claims of every Christian writer or preacher always and everywhere have been indisputably true by the judgement of historians or scientists, Christians have become a little humbler and a little less self-assertive. There can be an intellectual and spiritual asceticism as well as a merely physical habit of self-denial. We can learn to 'travel light' on our pilgrimage, not by disloyalty to old truths, but in a spirit of quietness. Argument is not the only way of defending the faith; and when it is poorly conducted, as it often has been, it is a good way of damaging the faith. If a philosopher tells us that we can not logically believe in an all-powerful loving God since his existence is denied by the suffering of his creation, there is no need to bluster, nor to say *anything* in reply. In so far as it is true, the statement must be accepted with intellectual humility. In so far as it is only part of the truth, we learn more of it from silence, from the lives of the suffering transformed by the Passion of Jesus Christ, the ultimate mystery of Calvary, the most violent and eloquent example in history, according to theology, when the power of God was seemingly abandoned, and his Love was most totally vulnerable.

'The generation that asks for a sign is a wicked and unfaithful generation' (Matthew 12:39), and our unfaithful generation has asked for signs and received them. Just as the believer is

compelled to recognise the unpalatable truth of many dis-
coveries by sceptical inquirers, so the unbeliever is faced with
the bare fact of miracle taking place in our midst. I have never
seen or witnessed a miracle. But even if one allows for the fact
that almost all miracle stories are pious exaggerations, or
simple lies, there remain certain things in our time which can
not be denied or argued away. I think for instance of the
stigmata in the body of Padre Pio, an Italian friar who suffered
wounds in his hands and his feet and his side, exactly parallel to
the wounds of Christ. There are many people alive now who
saw him. All the medical reports are agreed that the wounds
could not have been self-inflicted, and there is no way of
explaining why they remained fresh and open without healing, and without becoming septic. Indeed, many eye-
witnesses have testified that there came from the body of the
saint the very odour of sanctity, a smell like flowers. If one
read this story in a medieval legendary one would reject it as
the wildest fantasy. But it has happened in our midst, and all
attempts to prove that it was faked up have been abortive. I say
nothing of the extraordinary stories of Padre Pio's 'bi-
location', his gifts of being seen in two places at once; nor of
the various 'miracles' attributed to him. Again, one has to
recognise the phenomenon in our times of Lourdes. Few of the
many cures there have been claimed as miraculous by the
authorities; but some defy ordinary scientific explanation.
Nor is Lourdes the only place, nor is the Roman Catholic
Church the only religious group, in which there have happened fully accredited miracles in our own time, witnessed by
dispassionate observers who have been unable to explain
them. I think of a priest of the Church of England that I was
lucky enough to know. After his death, I heard the story of
how he had anointed the eyes of a baby born blind. The
Moorfields Eye Hospital in London declared that there was
nothing which could be done to restore the child's sight since
its optic nerves were dead. But, immediately after the annoint-
ing, the child was found to have perfect sight. And the priest,
in imitation of Another, charged them to speak of it to no one.
(Mark 7:36). As in the Gospel, they were unable wholly to

keep it to themselves, which is how I came to hear the story. There are many such miracles of healing in all the churches, and many more 'unexplained' recoveries from illness or sudden inflowings of strength as a result of the church's ministry of healing. One should be cautious about claiming miracles as 'an argument in favour of religion'. If a faithless generation would not believe Moses and the prophets, they would not believe though one can be raised from the dead. But equally, it would be unhistorical and unscientific not to recognise that, at the very least, there are unexplained phenomena in our midst, things which admit of no 'rational' explanation.

Saint Augustine, who devotes a chapter of his *City of God* to miracle-stories, asks, 'What do these miracles attest but the faith which proclaims that Christ rose in the flesh, and ascended into heaven with the flesh?' A good reproof to me, with my doubting Thomas's attitude to the story of the Ascension in Saint Luke. Augustine then goes on to point out that miracles are *signs*; that is what the word means; and that an equally great sign is to be seen in the death of martyrs.

It was in bearing witness to this faith that the martyrs endured the bitter enmity and savage cruelty of the world; and they overcame the world not by resisting but by dying.

In our own century, also, we have seen men and women martyred for the Christian faith. The quality of the deaths of, say, Dietrich Bonhoeffer or Maximilian Kolbe at the hands of the Nazis is an inspiration to set beside the moments of intellectual difficulty which Christians might feel in the West, cocooned from the experiences which Saint Augustine describes. In the Soviet labour camps to this hour, Christians are offering their lives with a dedication which fills the world with awe. Though one can make too heavily the point that Christianity only flourishes in times of persecution; though one can make melodramatic the contrast between the vigorous Christianity of the East and the pampered, privileged watered-down Christianity of the West, the survival and revival of the Church in Russia is one of the most remarkable facts of the last thirty years. Not all the most interesting or heroic people to have emerged from Russia since the second world war have been Christians. There have been many heroic Jews, atheists and others. But the Christian testimony is not easy to escape.

Much more modestly, however, anyone who now calls himself a Christian carries in his or her head 'a great cloud of witnesses', of those who in various ways have helped them to the faith. It may be a Christian one has read about in a book, or someone known to us personally. Almost everyone who has been 'put off' Christianity will say that they were disillusioned by the lives of Christians they knew. It is very rare if mere analysis or argument makes someone lose their faith. They nearly always supply the arguments having found individual manifestations of Christianity repulsive. In the same way, but by contrast, almost all those who call themselves Christians would say that they owed their faith, under God, to another person. This fact should give every self-confessed Christian pause. But it is not worth asking oneself: 'Am I behaving in a way calculated to make any honest inquirer abandon the quest? Or am I a light in the world?' The lights in the world never know that they are lights; those most certain of their own illuminating qualities are almost certainly the most repulsive.

Nevertheless, the quality of good Christian lives can not be ignored. It is for that reason, the light of Christ burning in them, that we revere saints. Their lives show that when a human being consecrates himself or herself utterly to Christ, the ideals of the Sermon on the Mount are not unattainable. Saint Martin of Tours gives his cloak to the beggar; Saint Francis embraces the leper, Saint Thérèse of Lisieux, with the greatest simplicity, became as the lilies of the field and – one of the strangest 'signs' to the world in the last hundred years, in spite of her completely hidden, very short and largely 'pointless' existence – she remains an inspiration to millions of wholly disparate and different people.

It is not merely, however, in reverence for the saints that one sees the light of Christ in other people's lives. He shines in the hearts of those who are very far from being saints. In some moods I have been helped by the faithful witness of those who would not abandon their faith in Christ Crucified, even though their unruly wills and affections were still chaotically out of control. There is much to be learnt from the humility of sinners, as well as from the sublimity of saints; sinners who are genuinely like the publican in the parable, standing far off and praying for God's mercy, picking themselves up again before the next dreadful lapse. Perhaps most Christians are really like this, though many lack the humility I am talking about. For the quality of a humble sinner's life preaches the same message as that of the saint. In so far as the failing has occurred it is not because Christ's teaching was wrong, but because the will was weak. 'Blame me – I do that myself – but blame *me* and not the path I tread'.

In fact, whether they are 'successes' or 'failures', Christian lives are the most potent sign of Christ in any generation; stronger, certainly, than miracles or arguments or decrees. For perhaps the most extraordinary thing of all about the teachings of Christ is that they turn out to be so ordinary. It sounds like a programme of pure madness. But when one looks about, one discovers that it is the sanest of one's friends who believe in it. The Sermon on the Mount only sounds paradoxical because the values of the secularist are so crazy. The only way to live in the world is by turning the values of the world on its head. We discover, as Christ's teaching is applied to human life, that it is not so much an impossible ideal after which only lunatics would aspire, but a factual analysis of human character which it would be insane to reject. A saying such as 'Lay not up for yourselves treasure on earth' seems impracticable until we contemplate the next sentence, 'Where your treasure is, there will be your heart also'. This is simply a statement of fact. And one sees what happens when the hearts of individuals, and of societies, become seduced by money. It is an ugly, but also a completely pathetic sight. Is it sane that one's happiness should depend on the strength of the dollar, or the price of gold, or the mystic number of the Dow Jones index? Is it sane to be tortured with fear that some share certificates, mere pieces of paper, might be 'worth' less than we paid for them? The great world of money, which makes so many people so unhappy is largely out of our control. A few bankers and brokers may believe that they know about the money supply. But no politician or economist has yet managed to prove that he can control 'market forces'. They claim to be in control of 'inflation' – but who believes them? If money is our god, and money worries are allowed to be dominant in our lives, we shall always be the prisoner of our treasure, whether we are merely sleepless in our beds because we are behind with the hire purchase payments, or frantic for news of multi-million 'deals' in the furthest corners of the earth. 'Where your treasure is, there will your heart be also'. The crazy few who have managed to shuffle off all possessions and all money have achieved a liberty which is unknown to those who have to pay bills and worry about bank balances.

The pursuit of power, gratification, experience, and pleasure seem perfectly natural, decent things until we give ourselves up to them. I remember once hearing a highly ascetic preacher saying that we should only 'give things up' for Lent in a spirit of pure sacrifice, and not because giving things up was good for us. It would be wrong to give up smoking purely for the sake of one's health, or to give up rich meals purely for the sake of losing weight. I did not follow his drift. I felt he could have seized upon the much more obvious truth that Christianity is physically good for you, as we should expect from one who said that he came as a physician to the sick. It has taken medical science two thousand years to discover the truth of what the itinerant exorcist said to his Galileean companions, that 'the life is a greater gift than food', and that health of the body is impossible to those who have not achieved serenity of mind. 'Can any of you, for all his anxiety, add a cubit's growth to his height?' Jesus did not teach puritanism. He drank wine, and he ate good meals, if the Gospels are to be believed. But as with money, so with physical gratification we are asked not to set our hearts upon them. 'It is for the heathen to busy themselves over such things; you have a Father in heaven who knows that you need them all'.

I believe that the closer one tried to follow these commandments of Christ, in a spirit of humility and quietness, the more one would find them to be simply true. It is only timidity which holds us back. It is our failure to keep the commandments, and not the wrongness of the commandments, which produces the turmoil in our divided hearts.

These, then, are the signs, which give an unbeliever pause in our world, and make him feel whether after all he is entitled to reject the Christ: miracle, martyrdom, sanctity, the quality of good Christian lives, and the sheer sanity, when further examined, of the words of Jesus. But the mysterious thing is that all these things can be considered, and the unbeliever will still remain an unbeliever. Perhaps the greatest weakness in the idea that God is a mere 'internalization' of our highest spiritual values is the implication that this is a matter fully dependent on our will. The unbeliever will never be able to deify, by artificial wish, what he knows or believes to be merely his own thoughts. 'Christ . . . made God his only idol. That may appear to come to the same thing, but to make God one's idol and to make one's idol God are two contrary movements'. It is only possible to make sense of the word God, to speak of God, to believe in God, or to know God, if, as well as being enthroned in our hearts, he is also recognised as a being outside ourselves. Many Christians have experienced this coming of God from the outside, often unwanted, into their lives.

> Amiable agnostics will talk cheerfully about 'man's search for God'. To me, as I then was, they might as well have talked about the mouse's search for the cat.

That was C. S. Lewis's bluff way of describing the moment of his conversion. It can be matched by countless testimonies, none of which would mean anything at all to an unbeliever. For the rational atheist, these stories of God himself – the Creator of heaven and earth, choosing to communicate with finite little mortals must seem the most ridiculous part of the Christian religion. Dean Inge, a colder fish than C. S. Lewis, nevertheless believed 'the immediate revelation of God to the human soul' as being the very ground of his faith.

Remembered revelation always tends to clothe itself in mythical or symbolic form. But the revelation was real; and it is here and here only – in the mystical act *par excellence*, the act of prayer – that faith passes for a time into sight. . . . But for the testimony of the great cloud of witnesses, who have mounted higher and seen more, I should not have ventured to build so much on this immediate revelation of God to the human soul. But the evidence of the saints seems to me absolutely trustworthy; and the dimness of my own vision would be disquieting only if I felt I had deserved better.

In another place, Inge addressed himself precisely to the question of whether God was *really* external to us, and concluded that the Christian life only begins when the external God has become internalized, when the Creator, who is responsible for the dawning of the religious consciousness in every human heart, has been welcomed into the heart. Both impulses are necessary – the recognition that God is *there*, and the welcoming him as the guest.

It is very significant how in its most inspired moments the human spirit falls into contradictions such as 'I, yet not I'; 'Work out your own salvation for it is God that worketh in you'. 'Thou couldest not seek Me', Pascal seemed to hear God saying to him – 'Thou couldest not seek me, hadst Thou not already found Me'. Yes, the externality of the voice of God in our hearts is not a fact with which faith can rest content. Salvation is not perfected in mere obedience or surrender. It consists rather in that full and final consecration to the purposes of God which can only exist when those purposes have become fully and finally our own.

★

The reality of this extraordinary experience, of God coming to us and making his presence unambiguously clear is in the end something which no word can describe and no joy can excel. Where all other frenzied aspirations and ambitions bring agitation and unhappiness, this visitation brings calm and peace. It does not transform the world, if by that is understood sweetening it, or removing its uglinesses, afflictions and miseries. On the contrary, it brings a clearer realism, but a realism tinged with the joyful sense that 'ere God made us He loved us; which love was never slacked, nor ever shall be.' (*Revelations of Divine Love*: Julian of Norwich). Saint Augustine of Hippo has described his slow conversion with the same joy bursting through the pathos and penitence of his words:

> Too late came I to love thee, O thou Beauty both so ancient and so fresh, yea too late came I to love thee. And behold, thou wert within me, and I out of myself, where I made search for thee: I ugly rushed headlong upon those beautiful things thou hast made. Thou indeed wert with me; but I was not with thee: these beauties kept me far enough from thee: even those, which unless they were in thee, should not be at all. Thou calledest and criedst unto me, yea though even breakedst open my deafness: thou discoveredst thy beams and shinedst unto me, and didst chase away my blindness: thou didst most fragrantly blow upon me, and I drew in my breath and I pant after thee; I tasted thee, and now do hunger and thirst after thee; thou didst touch me, and I even burn again to enjoy thy peace.

This is the Christian experience, not merely in dramatic conversions from unbelief, but in the little daily reconversion which takes place when the soul turns to God in prayer. Sooner or later, the experience of Christian prayer becomes an encounter with a person, an encounter which is so widely attested, so frequently experienced, that it would be bold to dismiss it as a delusion. The fruits of this delusion are 'love, joy, peace, patience, kindness, generosity, forebearance, gentleness, faith, courtesy, temperateness, purity' (Galatians 5.22). That alone ought to make one take the delusion seriously. They are qualities thin on the ground these days, and their possession has brought great happiness not only to the faces of those who exemplify them, but to all who have met these faces shining with Christ.

But it is neither a puzzle, nor an intellectual problem. It might begin as one. And the experience, once had, does not preclude the possibility that it might continue as one. Saint Paul's letters are the outpourings of a man who had seen the risen Lord, a vision of the triumphant and crucified saviour, but they are not the encyclicals of a man who has worked out all the answers. The difficulties remain, none greater than the problem of how the love of God allows or penetrates the pointless suffering of his creation. But the experience of God is not to be denied. It is easy enough to believe that anyone who turns to him in prayer would find him. They would find what they had been looking for. No father, if asked by his son for bread, would give him a stone. But the mystery is greater than that. Saint John said that we love God because he first loved us (I John 4:19), and Saint Paul (Romans 5:9) that while we were still sinners, Christ died for us. The dawn of our knowledge of God comes from God himself. It prompts one person to begin the quest, and another to reject it. We will have gone far along the road, probably, before we start to guess the end of the journey or the identity of our companion on the pilgrimage. But when his identity is recognised, as it has been and is by countless believers, the experience is unmistakable. Every believer could echo Saint Augustine's cry to God: 'Thou hast created us for thyself, and our heart cannot be quieted, till it may find repose in thee'.